King of Clubs
Maureen Prest

route

First published by Route in 2017
PO Box 167, Pontefract, WF8 4WW
info@route-online.com
www.route-online.com

ISBN : 978-1901927-70-2

Maureen Prest asserts her moral
right to be identified as the author of this book.

Thanks to:
Maureen's cousin 'Our Val' whose
pester power drove her to write *King of Clubs*.
And to Nancy Daley for the early read.

Cover Design:
GOLDEN
www.wearegolden.co.uk

Typeset in Bembo by Route

Printed and bound by CPI Group (UK) Ltd,
Croydon, CR0 4YY

Dedicated to my dearest friend
Pauline A Ellis
1946-2016

Introduction

King of Clubs is the story of a Yorkshire showman who had ideas above his station, so far above his station that his ideas knew no bounds. With a philosophy of 'Think Big', he was to bring the brightest stars that ever shone in the world of show business to his native Yorkshire. They were the jewels he wanted for his crown, the crown he was to place firmly on his head as the king of show business.

Much has been written about James Lord Corrigan and the Batley Variety Club, but where previous authors have devoted their works to the riches he generated and the fame which followed, as a close friend and confidant, I would like to tell his amazing personal story. In reaching for the stars he paid the highest price, not just in terms of money, but at a great cost to his personal life and his family.

James always maintained a strong work ethic. Born to a travelling fairground family, his childhood was too short; the Corrigans endured hardships most could not imagine. Life was grindingly harsh in pre-war England but, despite the austerity and lack of formal education, he came shining through. He had an overdose of charisma, his manners were impeccable, his appetite for life insatiable and he had an extra-large sense of humour. This was J L Corrigan, a special man who could charm the birds out of the trees. He changed millions of lives by giving people something to smile about, a reason to put on the glad rags and be entertained. He was a showman extraordinaire and sprinkled stardust for all to share.

Maureen Prest

Chapter 1

Penny Arcade

Overleaf: The Corrigan brothers. (L to R) Joey, John Edwin, James.

James Lord Corrigan was born on 20th August 1925 in Filey, North Yorkshire, to a well-known fairground family: the Corrigans. He could have been born anywhere, provided there was a town able to accommodate the travelling funfair.

James was the youngest of three brothers born to Mary and Joseph Corrigan. His eldest brother was named John Edwin, Joey came next, and then James. Mary had a son before she married, he was called Joe too. Their childhood was spent travelling the countryside with the close-knit and guarded fairground families.

Much of young James's education was at the knee of his grandfather, Joseph Michael Corrigan, a hard man and an old skinflint who was wise in the ways of the world. His knowledge and business skills were to prove a lasting influence on his youngest grandson. He was not a kind man, in fact he would be judged as cruel by today's standards. He would line the boys up and ask, 'Who would like a penny?' He'd then drop a coin to the ground and as the boys bent to pick it up he would kick them where it hurt. Perhaps it was their grandfather's way of toughening them up for their future survival. He did have a softer side to him though; a member of the family later revealed he would often walk past James's caravan, throw half a crown through the door and tell James's mother to buy food for the kids with it.

Joseph Michael was a well-respected member of the fairground community, a band of showmen detached from conventional society, travelling England, keeping themselves to themselves, and entertaining the masses. Grandfather Joseph held for a time the honour of being the chairman of The Showmen's Guild of Great Britain and was often mentioned in *World's Fair*, a newspaper published for showpeople.

His grandchildren were brought up in the same tradition as himself, for the ways of the world for a showman are just as the description suggests: all show. He was always looking for an opportunity to attract the public to something new. When an idea for a new attraction was thought up, you had to put the wisdom of old Grandfather Corrigan into action. His philosophy was 'go where the chimney pots are': the more chimney pots, the more houses, the more the population. He believed that you should always give good value for money. In those tough times money was earned the hard way and people had to be tempted to part with it. This is where James came into his own, for even as a young boy he studied hard how to attract a crowd.

The Corrigans travelled the countryside, living in caravans in the summer months, working steadily with the fair, going from one town to the next, pulling down the stalls and rides only to re-erect them a day or two later in a new town. It was a tough life and everyone pitched in to do their share, even the young. There was always work to be done keeping the stalls clean and bright, everything had to twinkle and sparkle. That way you attracted the crowds.

The Corrigans spread joy and a sense of fun. The children got excited when they saw the wagons trundling into the neighbourhood; the fairground rides and the swings all being erected for this one week of the year when they could have a good time spending their precious pennies. A trip to the fair brought welcome relief from the harsh realities of life. It was a land of make-believe in pre-war England. The music was deafening, steam engines piped music so loud the children wanted to follow. The fair spelled happiness. The smells of toffee apples, candy floss and brandy snap wafted through the air.

The fair had a planned route through the towns of Yorkshire and Lincolnshire. This was the routine until the long tour's end in Hull, a city on the east coast of Yorkshire. Not only did Hull spell the end of the season, it was a very profitable town to work. All the fairground families worked Hull and the Corrigans had their own special spot to pitch their stalls. Woe betide anyone who challenged them for it. This was their own spot, a pot of gold at the end of the rainbow that gave them enough money to eek out the winter months.

Nearby Filey was a favourite winter resting place for the tired Corrigans. These months were spent painting and renewing the rides, giving everything a general spruce up ready for the next season. Children of the families were now able to attend school, but life for a travelling child proved doubly hard. In school it was open season on the travellers, who were at the mercy of the local children's bullying and name calling. To grow up with these problems was to make or break a young child. James had the skin of an elephant and coped well with the taunts and jibes.

In school, James had his travelling friends to back him up, and their numbers ensured their safety; any attempt to single one out meant they had to tackle all. When there was a threat to the family, the ranks would close and inner protection was the order of the day. They would never let each other down. Sticking together was a secret of their great strength.

The extended fairground family suffered together and they celebrated together. Competition though was great amongst them, each striving for his own success. When some small achievement was gained, it was greeted with respect by all. To succeed was of paramount importance amongst their peers. The Corrigan's had the particular knack of giving the public what they wanted and providing value for money.

Mary, James's mother, would stand for hours at a stall where the customers would come to roll down their pennies. Her friend Janie Anne, a mother of three, had a wagon next to theirs. They were great friends, the kids being best pals for Mary's bunch. They lived in big wagons whose engines were constantly kept running to power the generators which provided the juice to illuminate the lamps and the fancy, beaded shades that attracted the punters to have a flutter on the many stalls. Janie Anne's stall was a 'Hook-a-duck'. The players bought a cane with a hook on the end and got three chances of hooking a lucky duck. On the underside of each duck was a message which read 'win' or 'lose'.

There were more losers than winners and the prize they won would be a cheap pot dog or a plastic whistle, despite the many exciting prizes surrounding the stall. They were there simply to lure the players in; no one ever won them, but the people enjoyed the challenge.

One night the biggest loser of all was Janie Anne. She put her three children to bed for the night, tucking them up warm in a corner of the wagon before going to work on her stall. When she returned, she opened the wagon door only to be choked back by fumes. Coughing and gasping for air, she dragged her children out one by one before collapsing on the ground. Her children were all dead, killed by the poisonous gases which had been leaking into the wagon for hours. The fairground came to a standstill. The tragedy was a great loss to the close community. A huge shadow was cast over the travelling families and a tragic lesson was learned by all. The mothers never again left their children in wagons unattended.

After the loss of Janie Anne's family, Mary wrapped her children in big overcoats to keep them warm as they slept under her stall, never letting them out of her sight. They were often cold, sometimes hungry, but they were always safe. When the stall closed for the night she woke them and put them to bed. James never forgot how she protected them. She was a wonderful mum. Long after she passed away, her photograph in a beautiful frame with a posy of fresh flowers took pride of place in his home as an homage to his mother.

The clouds of war were gathering in 1939. Life was changing for the whole country as men were being enlisted into the armed forces. John Edwin joined up, enlisting as a bomb disposal engineer. Joey also did his patriotic duty by joining the army. James was now fourteen but he too went; lying about his age he joined the Merchant Navy and became a wireless operator. Before he could start to learn Morse code, he had to first learn the alphabet, as his education had been little more than a teacher giving him a pencil and paper, telling him to 'sit in the corner and draw a picture'. The schools had no time for the travelling families, they would be gone before they had an opportunity to learn anything. Despite this, his dogged determination overcame any obstacle. And here he was, a young lad of fourteen, going to sea, dodging the torpedoes of the German Navy and ferrying much needed goods across the oceans to keep the country going.

He melted into the Navy life, living by his wits and keeping his head down. He may have been a young boy when he joined the Navy, but the hardships of war turned him into a man of the world. He survived everything the war threw at him and when peace was declared, he returned to his family, stronger, wiser and different.

Unfortunately, John Edwin had sustained a head injury caused by shrapnel whilst defusing a bomb and he was never to be the same again. Joey was blinded and sent home. James returned unscathed, more fortunate than his brothers, and was ready to resume the life of a showman. Soon after their return his two older brothers left the fair, going their own separate ways, leaving James to carry on the family tradition. He was now a very good-looking young man with jet black hair, a shock of which fell over an ever-smiling face. He was of medium height, well built, with an eye for the ladies.

The fair arrived in Batley, a grimy mill town in the heart of West Yorkshire. There were lots of chimneys there, with giant mill chimneys belching out smoke and soot. The sirens would wail out at six in the morning, summoning the mill workers to their chores. They worked amid the noisy clatter of machines, churning out endless miles of woollen cloth.

Alongside the woollen mills were 'the rag holes', correctly called the 'Shoddy & Mungo' mills. These housed a process whereby old rags were ground down to make reconstituted fabrics, the material used for carpet underfelts and the like. The mills employed the young ladies of the town to sort out the different material. It was a dirty job but nothing was wasted back in those days, every household had a rag bag. When the rag and bone man trundled down the streets on his horse and cart calling out for 'any old rags', the children would hastily find anything which would gain a penny to take to the corner shop for sweets. Everything was recycled, empty jam jars were washed and saved, the corner shop would buy them and send the clean glass back to be melted down only to re-emerge time after time. Everything was precious, nothing wasted. The war had brought with it rationing and though the war was now over, the rationing was to continue for many years. There were no luxuries. To put it bluntly, there were not enough necessities, food was scarce and the people of England existed on the barest of essentials.

Batley was surrounded by a series of grim towns that merged into one: Wakefield, Dewsbury, Huddersfield, Leeds, Halifax, Bradford, Brighouse; a giant caldron of conurbations belching out smoke from the furnaces which powered the machinery of the industrial north. The workers of these towns lived in endless rows of terraced houses, laughingly called two-up two-down. These back-to-back dwellings each had an obligatory tin bath hung on the wall outside the house ready to be used on a Friday night to wash away the grime of the week from the oily mills. There were no bathrooms, the toilets were usually at the bottom of the yard or through a ginnel and shared with others. The householders took it in turns to keep them clean. The pathways and steps leading to the privy were scrubbed every week and white scouring rubbed on the step edges, denoting in darkness where to step. Cleanliness was everything to the people of Yorkshire, together with their own particular brand of friendliness.

Grandad Corrigan was right to say go where the chimney pots are; to arrive in Batley was to attract the occupants away from the drudgery of their lives and divert them into the fleeting joys of the fair; any diversion from their circumstances was a relief. The people flocked to the muddy fairground to have a go on everything in sight; roundabouts, swings and the amazing Shamrock and Columbia, a huge pair of boats which would almost swing full circle, giving the riders a feeling of sickness

16

all in the name of fun. The dodgems and waltzers played their part in the excitement.

Batley was not a town the Corrigan family enjoyed visiting, for it was here where James's great, great grandfather was killed in a pub brawl. The fair hit the headlines for all the wrong reasons and, from that day forward, the Corrigans were strictly teetotal. Keeping with the family tradition, James never drank alcohol.

The town may have been unlucky in the past for the Corrigans but it was to prove lucky for him, as James met Betty Wimpenny, a local girl. She was very pretty with dark hair and an engaging laugh. He was besotted, as was she. Their relationship was frowned upon by her family; a 'feaster' was hardly a suitable partner for the daughter of a Wimpenny. Despite all the objections, nothing was to deter them from being married. Their wedding took place in 1949 at the parish church in Hanging Heaton, a little hamlet on the edge of Batley. They were grateful for the few wedding gifts they received on the happy day and, despite the deep depravation, they managed to get a home together with help from family and friends. Once married, James's fairground days came to an end. At the age of twenty-four, his new life began.

Chapter 2

The Hungry Years

Overleaf: James in Canada.

The newly married couple settled for a little home in Leeds. This was a first for James, he now had an address following a lifetime being of 'no fixed abode'. James and Betty had firm ideas as a go-ahead young couple. Neither was afraid of hard work and they were ambitious to improve their lot. Their early days together were a very happy time, building a future for themselves away from both their early beginnings.

In 1953 they were blessed with a baby son. They named him James but he was forever to be called Jamie so as not to be confused with his father. With a happy family unit, James was always looking for inspiration for a new venture. He tried many things to make ends meet but nothing really clicked. After a period of trial and error, he and Betty decided to up sticks and emigrate to Canada. They arrived in Toronto in 1956 with very little money but with huge hopes for a prosperous future and a better way of life than the one they had left behind.

James got a job selling real estate. Looking the part with his newly acquired suit and briefcase, he set out to make a success of himself, shedding the image of the fairground man and acquiring a smooth, well-spoken manner; he sounded more like a product of Eton College than a rough and ready travelling man. He could charm the birds out of the trees and his happy disposition was infectious, all necessary skills for the success he and Betty wanted for themselves in this new country. The world of commerce was no different to that of the penny arcades. Money was money, even if it was made differently; the end result was the same.

One day, James saw an advertisement for a cameraman at a TV studio. He applied for the job, telling them he had a wealth of experience gained in the mother country. He landed the job, not knowing one end of a TV camera from the other, but he had enough nouse about him to believe he could fake it and so it was. He spent many months as a successful cameraman for a Canadian broadcasting organisation. He was a workaholic, selling encyclopaedias in his spare time. Anything to make money.

James and Betty made a good team. With a young son to care for, Betty's time was limited. She could not go out to work, instead she spent her days with Jamie. She soon became homesick for England and the life she had left behind. Betty pined for her mum Sally, her brother Barry and her sister Mary. They all missed each other. Betty was also missing the extended family for her young son. James also longed to be back in England. They had dreamed of making their fortune in Canada, but alas, they made a good living but little else. They decided to save money to travel back to England.

They hit on a novel idea to earn extra money. When James finished work at the TV station, they all went to a local golf course and, after dark, would dig for worms. It was crawling with them, they had a never ending supply. They sold the worms to local fishermen as bait for their hooks. Saving hard, they earned enough money to return back to England, eventually arriving back in October 1958 with £3 and five shillings in their pockets.

James, Betty and Jamie went to stay with Sally, Betty's mum in Batley, until they could make enough money to get started again. Whilst not taking Canada by storm, they arrived back in the UK with a newly acquired confidence and were a very attractive, happy young couple with strong, dark good looks, well spoken, well mannered, and prepared for hard work. They loved being back amongst their own people who they loved and understood. They settled down rebuilding their lives, their wanderlust well and truly satisfied.

Always trying to think of the next big idea, the ever–resourceful James noticed the terraced houses in and around the mill towns were being spruced up by having their windows leaded. Indeed, if one house had the improvement of leaded windows, you could guarantee the neighbours were not to be outdone and they would follow suit. Given the number of houses in and around Batley, the world was his oyster. He got to work, bought a ladder and taught himself the art of window leading. After walking around the streets of Batley, knocking on doors and launching his charm offensive, it took him no time at all to convince the housewives of the benefit of having leaded windows. In reality, they offered no benefit whatsoever other than decoration, but he soon got his new business off the ground. He made it a great success and provided well for Betty and Jamie.

There were times in the winter months when he'd arrive home with his hands bleeding from the brittle glass and lead. He carried on despite his acute discomfort until they were able to save enough money to buy a little cottage that was once owned by Betty's grandfather, who had hanged himself in the parlour before Betty was born. It was special to Betty as she had been born there in an area of Batley called Soothill. 'Oaks Cottage', as she named it, sat at the end of Oaks Road. It dated back to 1450, was a two-up one-down, and stood in its own ground. There was no bathroom or kitchen, it was a shell of a place that was run down and badly in need of modernising. They managed to buy it for £400.

Betty welcomed the challenge of turning it into their home. All the money James earned was ploughed into it. Betty had vision and flair and a talent for the unusual. Her plan was to turn it into a 'hacienda type house' with shutters by the windows. Of course, the windows were leaded by James in a diamond pattern. The stucco walls were painted white, the shutters painted black, it was their little palace. The home would grow as their fortunes grew, little by little.

The latest craze to sweep the towns and villages was bingo. James was no stranger to the game of chance, he knew how to operate such a business; it was nothing new to a showman. He had been brought up with lotto or 'housey-housey' as it was called in the fairgrounds. He and Betty secured a lease on a large room over the Conservative Club in Batley. Being big enough to accommodate a few hundred people, they judged it a good opportunity to make some serious money. No more sore hands for James, he swapped his ladders for a microphone and he and Betty ran their own bingo hall which they called Victoria Bingo. It was to be the turning point to a more lucrative life and different to anything they had ever known.

The bingo craze took off in a big way and the ladies of the West Riding would leave their husbands babysitting while they went out for a night at the bingo in the hope of returning home with a few extra pounds to help out with the housekeeping, having fun in the process. Bingo was here to stay, so much so that it was fast becoming big business.

In the Victoria, James was in his element, chatting to the lady members, oozing charm and keeping them entertained as only a true showman knows how. He was endowed with a charisma which could win over the most disenchanted of patrons. He would have them laughing in no time, which in itself was a great talent. The bingo players came flocking in.

Betty and James loved the life and, most of all, the financial gains. Being back amongst their own people meant everything to them. These were the people they understood and who understood them. The Yorkshire people were hard working and loved nothing more than to see people 'get on' if they were prepared to roll up their sleeves and work. These two young people could not be accused of shirking; if they were not at the bingo hall they were to be found re-dressing second-hand bricks, stacking them in piles ready to be used to add another room to a house which was growing slowly but surely.

Betty was no stranger to the pick and shovel. She too would give it her all. She noticed an old rag shed adjoining their land at the corner of the road and thought it could be turned into a garage. She went with James to meet the owners and, after much haggling, they bought the old wreck and added it to their property. They had never been inside the old tumbledown so

James and Betty approached it with a hammer to break off the rusted padlock. James shattered the lock in one fell swoop. As they opened the door, shedding light on the old, dilapidated building, much to their surprise it was filled with sacks of old rags. They looked like they had been there forever and smelled like it too. It was stacked to the rafters. 'Oh God,' Betty thought, 'What are we going to do with this lot?' They started clearing them out.

Later that night they almost collapsed after the exertion of the day. First James started scratching, then Betty, and before long they were hopping around the room. They had been infested with fleas. Betty grabbed a bottle of DDT, a favourite insect killer of the day. She doused them both with it before getting in the bath together to wash each other free of the invading parasites. They were absolutely crawling. The following day she rang Batley Council to send the fumigation team to treat the place before they could empty the contents of the building and turn it into the proposed double garage. She must have had an inkling their cars would one day be bigger than those they owned at the time; you could have housed two buses in the place. When it was eventually finished and rendered with the same stucco pattern as the house, it made a statement as you drove into the grounds of the now impressive property.

As a couple they worked well together. They laughed at the experience shared, the day they cleared the rags. They were wrapped up in their own little world as happy as anyone could be, always confiding their hopes and dreams to each other. Any business dealings were discussed together, each adding to the mix. They were a pair, they had a good head for business and knew they would go far. Indeed, they were determined to go far.

James was approached by an accountant by the name of Derek Ford who ran a travel agency in his home town of Castleford. Derek had been watching James's progress and invited him to be his partner in a proposed chain of bingo halls across Yorkshire. The two men were as different as chalk and cheese.

Derek was a stereotypical accountant, introverted and with not a great deal of personality. James on the other hand was the extrovert, charming, always smiling, and he had the Midas touch, everything he touched turned to gold. His star was very definitely in the ascendancy. Derek and James soon formed a company known as 'Corrigan Ford Enterprises'. This was to be the start of a very successful partnership.

Betty was never impressed with the partnership. When it was suggested that the Victoria should be rolled into Corrigan Ford Enterprises, she resisted, pointing out the lease was partly owned by her. She was not about to relinquish it, certainly not to benefit Derek Ford, who she could not abide. Betty and Derek were like oil and water, they could not mix, and she never missed an opportunity to voice her feelings to James.

To appease Betty, James signed his half of the Victoria Bingo business over to her. The bingo hall, which had brought them such good fortune, was now owned and run by Betty alone, with all the profits being ploughed into Oaks Cottage. Like Topsy, the house was growing, a wing was added, then another. It was furnished to perfection with the best money could buy. She bought adjoining land, enlarged the gardens and had them landscaped with a wall to enclose them from the other residents of Oaks Road. Their home was worthy of being featured in any periodical of homes with good taste and style, for Betty had good taste in abundance. She would hire builders, plumbers and decorators to put her ideas into action. She had a strong and forceful personality, woe betide anyone who did not pull their weight, she took no prisoners and became forceful to the point of being deeply unpopular.

At the heart of the house was the original cottage owned by Betty's grandfather. The room where her grandfather ended his days became the dining room. Betty considered herself as something of a psychic. She could feel a presence. She swears that one day a loaf of bread levitated up from the table and hovered about two feet in the air without any provocation. It stayed there for a few moments then simply dropped down with a thud. She believed her grandfather was an ever-present spirit who had gone into the afterlife deeply troubled and unable to gain a resting peace. Strange things happened in that house and visitors felt discomfort. This would highly amuse Betty, she would exaggerate the discomfort by relating ghostly goings on with a glint in her eye, knowing very well she was instilling fear into her guests. She would hold a Ouija session with anyone brave enough to join in, usually in the dining room. Betty was becoming obsessed with the paranormal and anxious to know what fate had in store.

James was going from strength to strength. Corrigan Ford Enterprises was to eventually acquire twenty-two bingo halls and three cinemas, a giant organisation which was a major company to run and control. Derek undertook the bulk of the responsibility for the day-to-day running from their headquarters at the Crystal Bowl in Castleford, a large bingo hall and amusement arcade with a suite of offices to accommodate the directors.

Trying to control a company as large as this held its own problems. A company turning over huge amounts of cash needed a constant eye on all the establishments. Derek and James had an army of detectives looking after their interests in the various towns, no one was above suspicion. Any manager caught with their fingers in the till was down the road quick as a flash. This happened on a regular basis.

James developed a highly suspicious personality which left him with no peace of mind. He would often have his premises bugged, listening in on conversations was an everyday occurrence in the running of his business. It reflected on every aspect of his daily life. If he wanted to have a private conversation with anyone, he would ask them to take a walk with him, usually outdoors, never staying in one place long enough for his words to be overheard. It was amusing and curious at the same time. He was deeply suspicious of everybody, no doubt thinking he could be overheard in much the same way as he had eavesdropped on others.

Derek, ever the accountant, would analyse to the last penny.

Unlike the Corrigans, his lifestyle was akin to a Quaker, spending very little. James on the other hand liked making money, but had very little regard for it. As far as he was concerned, it was the 'thrill of the chase'. During these heady days, he carried little money.

Life was busy but the Corrigans would occasionally take a night off, diverting themselves from the stresses of the business world. A supper club had opened in Wakefield called Kon-Tiki; it was a small, intimate club with a stage in one corner. Cabaret artistes would be engaged to perform and entertain the diners after their meal. It was a fairly expensive night out but special, somewhere to go to celebrate a special occasion. The concept impressed James and inspired him. What would there be to stop him building a club on a large scale, large enough to accommodate hundreds of people, a venue in the north of England? After all, everything good in the entertainment industry was in the south, London being the hub of the entertainment world. The north had nothing, there was only the odd working men's club staging a Saturday night turn! In those days *Sunday Night at the London Palladium* was the television highlight of the week and was the showcase of Britain's top talent. James's idea was to engage the top artistes from the world of show business to perform for the people of the north who had been starved of entertainment since the theatres had closed.

James kept turning the idea around in his head and, the more he thought about it, the more he was inspired by the concept. He talked it through with Betty. She was always an encouragement to him and this idea was no exception. She was intoxicated by James's enthusiasm. He asked her where they should build it and, quick as a flash, she said, 'Why, here in Batley of course.' The seed was sown. They flew to Las Vegas and did a tour of the show bars on the strip, saw a few shows and studied the format. They both decided how it should look; not as flashy as Vegas but a more sober approach to their club. Sums had been worked out as to how much seating capacity would be needed to make it a viable, profit-making business, big enough to pay the world-class stars but not too expensive to be out of reach of the patrons who would be their audience. They were excited at the prospect and became obsessed by the idea.

One day James arrived home.

'Betty, get your coat on.'

She asked why.

'I have found the land where we can build the club.'

He drove her to Bradford Road, ten minutes from their house. On the main road, between Batley and Dewsbury, he pulled up and said, 'It's here.' Betty looked in disbelief. The land was a disused sewerage works. 'Are you sure about this?' was her reply.

'Yes, never been surer, think about it, we are midway between Leeds, Huddersfield, Halifax, Wakefield, Bradford and Brighouse. How many chimney pots? Too many to count.'

Grandad Corrigan would most certainly approve.

James had to talk long and hard to convince Betty that a disused sewerage works was to be the site for their next big adventure. They sat in their car staring at the land as he convinced her of his logic.

'What shall we call it?' James asked.

'Batley Variety Club, what else?' replied Betty.

Not for them any pretentious, dreamed up title. They were proud of their town and its people, and this was a project for the people. The motorways were being built across the Pennines, opening up Lancashire. The M1 was being built from London, passing through Sheffield and Wakefield. They had a catchment of millions. It had to work. Betty was hooked. This was to be the start of what was to become the world famous Batley Variety Club.

Chapter 3
I Believe

Overleaf: Betty and Jamie in St Mark's Square, Venice.

The architects drew up the plans for the club with both Betty and James stipulating how it should look. Betty was good at designing and had her own ideas for the unique build they were about to embark upon. Working closely with the professionals, they arrived at what satisfied them both. They had lain awake for weeks talking and thinking it through. They were painstaking, so much thought and care had gone into this huge undertaking.

Eventually plans were submitted to Batley Council for their approval. They had their work cut out trying to convince the powers that be that the club would be good for the area. It may have been above the council's comprehension, who had no idea of the ambition and potential. Show business to them was the local amateur dramatics but, with the prospect of jobs for the local people, they were won over and permission was granted.

Once all the formalities were out of the way, James found a builder who would undertake the work. The couple took control of the build. Betty had her idea of how the interior was to look; she wanted the club to be excavated, that is to say, on entering, the public would walk down to their tables which would be arranged in tiers, five in all, forming a huge horseshoe embracing the stage from the bottom up, thus giving the audience unobstructed views. The building was to be wide without pillars. She remembered as a child being taken to a theatre and not seeing too much as she was in a seat behind a pillar. The building was to be low, thus offering an intimate atmosphere. The club would hold 1,750 people seated, with standing room for many more. The safety of such a large audience was of paramount importance. The fire brigade had to inspect the plans and all safety aspects. Fire escapes and a sprinkler system had to be incorporated.

The vast auditorium was to have a long bar at each side, running almost the whole length of the club. These bars were vital to the economic viability; it was always James's idea to use the bar takings as a way of keeping the admission costs down. He was hell bent on giving the public the best entertainment money could buy, at a cost the public could afford.

In the sixties, money was short; a man's wages in those days amounted to less than twenty pounds a week. If James was to fill the place on a nightly basis, only the top stars from the world of show business would be good enough for his audiences. His motto would be, 'Batley Variety Club, Where The World's Top Stars Play'. But if James was convinced he could attract artistes from all over the world, the vast majority of the public thought he was mad. When his plans were unfolded to the general public, they found it inconceivable that a scruffy little mill town would be the host to artistes of world renown. Here was someone who was about to blow stardust over the place where soot, dust and grime had blackened the buildings for generations. Not only that, but to build it on a disused sewerage bed was the most implausible part of the story. Well, if nothing else, it made for good copy.

The press were hooked. National newspaper reporters found their way to Batley with great difficulty, because no one had heard of this little town, but find it they did and James welcomed them with open arms. He was happy to benefit from the free publicity. The daily papers were writing about the man and his club. The story was being written alongside the build, which was a godsend because no one thought this gamble would pay off. Though it was the curiosity of the venture that attracted such great coverage, the press also wanted to be there when James Corrigan fell flat on his face. What they were not to know was there was always a Plan B. If his dream did not pay off he would turn it into a bingo hall. That was something he kept up his sleeve, not to be revealed.

The build finally begun with a deadline for completion of three months, from start to finish. A tall order. It was decided everyone would work day and night. Arc lights were erected and a shift system put in place.

To keep the publicity going, James and Betty hit on the idea of having a ceremony. A foundation stone would be laid, a tradition of the north, thus giving the building its identity and a certain amount of good fortune. They decided to get someone from the world of show business to perform the ceremony. The Bachelors, an Irish singing group, were in the hit parade and getting lots of television exposure when they were approached. Con Clusky, who was the lead singer in the outfit, said in a huffy kind of way, 'We do not perform in clubs, only in theatres.' James asked him what he would be likely to gain from a theatre engagement. Con revealed a figure.

'Well how about if I double that amount for the opening week at Batley?'

'Well in that case,' said Con, 'I think that can be arranged.'

A contract was signed for The Bachelors to perform on the opening week three months hence.

The Bachelors duly turned up to perform the foundation stone ceremony. James had talked a local brass band into playing them along the road from Batley town centre to the building site of the club, less than a mile. He hired an open-top limousine for himself, Betty and The Bachelors to be driven behind the band, at walking pace. The Bachelors were bemused; they had never been involved in anything like this before. James however knew exactly what he was doing. He was dragging the people out of their houses on to the streets of Batley to witness the sight of his first stars arriving to do his bidding. It was the talk of the town and that was exactly what he wanted. By now James was blazing a trail for the club.

TV cameras were searching him out for interviews and he was more than pleased to accommodate. His charm and enthusiasm was infectious, just as it had been behind the cameras in Canada. He knew the technique of the camera angles and used them to good effect, coming across to the viewers as a likeable dreamer. What was not appreciated was that Betty and James had done a great deal of homework on the costing and the presentation of their plan. James had worked out the seating capacity and had budgeted not for a capacity audience but for the costs to be covered on two-thirds full. He wanted to keep the admission fees as low as possible; five shillings and sixpence maximum (twenty-eight pence in today's money) unless it was a very great artist then the entry charge would be increased. The cost of a pint of beer was one shilling and six pence (eight pence today). The food was a basket meal, again costed to be within the working man's budget.

The people of Yorkshire were a downtrodden lot and they had been overlooked for years as the workhorse of the country. Knowing nothing of the world of glamour, it was inconceivable they would have on their doorstep the great and the good of the world of showbiz. They had never been showered with anything other than smoke and soot!

James and Betty worked as a team, which is what they had done all their married lives. This, the biggest of their dreams, was no exception. Between them they covered every detail; Betty was good at detail. James had the job of raising the money to make their dream a reality.

The build was on course when an inspector turned up from the local council. He measured up the site only to find the building was six feet too close to the road. This was catastrophic. What were they to do? How could such a mistake have been made? The builder was called. The architect was called. Everyone stood about scratching their heads at the situation they now found themselves in. Nevertheless, the council had to be obeyed and the necessary amendments were made. The new structure was pulled down and rebuilt, this time with the blessing of the building inspector, adding greatly to what were becoming astronomical costs.

James had not budgeted for any unforeseen complications and had to look for extra funding. He approached a local brewery. By this time, he was so well known he needed no introduction. He walked into the Scottish and Newcastle brewery having made an appointment with the directors. He was to offer them the opportunity of a lifetime. If they would loan him the substantial amount of money necessary to finish his build, he would permit them to sell their ales in his soon to be completed club. It did not take a genius to work out the size of the proposal. 1,750 seating capacity plus the standing room, also with the extended hours permitted for drinking, the brewery would be onto a winner. Caution being the watchword of Yorkshiremen, they wanted to know what would happen if the club failed as most people were predicting. James always being a man to have the answers ready before the question was asked, let them into the secret of Plan B. He came away with the funding he needed to complete the project and the loan was to be repaid at a very low interest rate.

James was elated. He drove back to Betty and told her the good news that the financial worry of the cost of completing the club had been overcome. She too was relieved as the costs, together with the initial mistakes, had mounted. They had sunk such a lot of money into the project she was beginning to worry if they had done the right thing in embarking on it. However, it was too late to entertain these thoughts now, they were in too deep to have any lasting regrets, so they bravely carried on making sure every little detail was covered and kept their spirits up by telling themselves all would be well in the end.

Despite having his work cut out with the day-to-day running of the bingo empire, James had to find an agent capable of booking the artistes to appear. For not only was there to be a star of the show, support acts would have to be engaged to give his future audiences an evening to remember and give them value for money. That was the only way to succeed in hard times. The format proposed was to have a compère and introduce a speciality act; a comic, a singer, etc. After much searching, James found theatrical agent Bernard Hinchcliffe. James took advice from Bernard and gave him the job of booking the support acts. He also helped find the best musicians in the area. To become resident was a godsend to musicians, who were not accustomed to working seven nights a week. This was real security for them. Despite the lacklustre nature of the area, it was more than blessed with musical talent. The musicians of Batley Variety Club could hold their own with the best of them; indeed it was to become clear they were amongst the greatest in the world.

Artistes had to be booked long before the completion of the build. Managements were approached and contracts signed. Any doubts about the suitability of the venue for the stars was swept aside by James who was not only prepared to pay the top fees, he was to afford them the dignity of their status as stars. He would build wonderful backstage facilities, something the old run-down theatres were woefully lacking; they were often mice infested, cold dressing rooms with a broken sink and cold tap, and a rusty nail banged into the wall to hang a hat and coat. That would not be the case in this purpose built theatre club. A suite was to be afforded to the top of the bill, consisting of a shower and dressing room with well-lit mirrors that opened out on to a sitting room with a comfortable sofa, coffee table and chairs, where the artistes could entertain and sign autographs. A row of clean, bright dressing rooms came next for the support acts, plus a band room for the musicians. This accommodation was to run almost the length of the building backstage, stopping to incorporate a huge kitchen from where the meals in a basket were to be cooked.

Mindful of keeping costs down, the catering was made as simple as possible. There was to be a choice of chicken and chips or scampi and chips, served with plastic forks. Disposal was convenient, everything was thrown into the bin thus avoiding any washing up. Also the plastic forks made no sound, a consideration when artistes performed so the background noise was kept to a minimum.

It was important to get the front of house finished first. The booking office was situated adjacent to the front doors. In the foyer, a large station was erected with plans of the auditorium so the public could choose and book their tables for the forthcoming shows. The club was due to open on 26th March 1967 and it was decided to open for bookings three weeks prior to a new show opening. Thus bookings were being taken for three shows at any given time. This was vital to the wealth of the club.

A second storey was built above the foyer, containing a manager's office, a general office, a safe room, control room and, most imposing of all, James L Corrigan's office. This opened out onto a balcony from where he could walk out and see the whole of the club. Positioned at both ends of the balcony were the lighting stations for the spotlight operators. All the stage lighting was controlled from here. A number of seats arranged for any special guests occupied the middle ground.

Betty took control of the décor for James's office. There was a huge oak desk with matching well-padded swivel chair and an intercom connecting him to all areas of the club. A plush carpet was fitted that you almost disappeared into, and it was furnished with a sumptuous squashy sofa and two equally sumptuous squashy chairs. Gold slub-satin curtains framed the huge window which looked out onto Bradford Road. A copy of Canaletto's 'Saint Mark's Square, Venice' was placed on the wall behind James's desk (James and Betty had taken a holiday there with Jamie). Two telephones sat side by side on his desk; one was a very private line, the other was a house line open to all. Outside his office there was an illuminated sign above a bell push. One sign said 'Enter', the other 'Engaged'. All very high-tech in the sixties. 'The Swinging Sixties' had very definitely swung past Batley, that is until now! Nothing was overlooked. No expense was spared.

The opening night grew ever closer, but the setbacks continued and the grand plan was falling behind schedule. At all costs they had to meet the deadline otherwise James and Betty would have been ruined. Not only had the first artistes been booked, but contracts had been signed for top artistes three months ahead. The forthcoming attractions had to be household names if the plan was to work. With the courage of his convictions and a giant leap of faith, James had committed them to a fortune. If the build faltered, or the people didn't come, they didn't have the money to pay for all they had committed to.

There was to be a million and one problems to solve, none more so than the licensing of the club. The laws then were an absolute carved in stone dictate: closure of all licensed premises by 10:30pm midweek, which could be extended to 11.00pm on a Saturday. Sunday, being the day of the Lord, meant all premises were closed by 10.00pm. The club needed to be open until midnight, so the only way these limits could be overcome was to turn the premises into a private members' club, which meant any future club goer had to become a member to gain entry. Application was made to the licensing authorities and granted. All that remained was to publish the rules in the press, together with a printed application form. The public were invited to apply for membership together with a small administration fee. On completion they became members for life. Whenever they visited the club they would have to show their membership card, otherwise entry could be denied. An ex-police officer was engaged to take charge of all membership applications.

The first sign as to how popular the club was to become was when the thousands of applications came flooding in – 70,000 before opening night. The post office in Batley made two trips a day delivering sacks of newspaper cut-out coupons, duly completed. This number eventually crept to over 300,000.

The opening ceremony was to take place on the afternoon of 26th March 1967, Easter Sunday. Four golden keys had been made for the ceremony, one for James and Betty to keep as a memento, one for Con of The Bachelors to unlock the club and mark the opening, plus one each for John Stokes and Dec Clusky the other two members of The Bachelors who were to top the bill on opening night.

The deadline day arrived. Everyone was dashing around putting the finishing touches to the club. James and Betty were on their hands and knees in the toilets laying the floor tiles. The piano which had been ordered had not arrived. This was the most magnificent instrument, a full concert grand made by the great Bechstein, the finest name in Saxony pianos. It had cost a fortune. As this was the star of any orchestra, Betty took it upon herself to get this vital piece of equipment delivered and on stage come what may. She made phone calls to establish what had held up the delivery and discovered it had been loaded onto a delivery truck but it had broken down on route to Batley. 'Where is it broken down?' she screamed down the phone at the unfortunate soul who took the call. It was times like these when she could strip paint with her tongue. She called a mechanic to get the stricken vehicle up and running post haste. He eventually got them back on the road. The piano was so big, it had to be dismantled for transportation and rebuilt again on arrival. A piano tuner was on standby to bring the instrument to life. There was an army of helpers at the back of the building, frantically working to get the piano in house and in place at the corner of the stage where it would sit forever more.

The house pianist was to be a genius by the name of Tony Cervi. He could play anything, with or without music. He was an enormous asset to the club, and had the pleasure of accompanying some of the greatest stars in show business. He was quietly spoken, very unassuming, and had the patience of a saint.

By this time Betty was exhausted. She had worked day and night, interviewing the attractive girls in the area who had applied for the jobs of waitresses. They queued around the block, anxious to get a job which paid three shillings and six pence an hour (eighteen pence in today's money). There was no shortage of applicants. Once given a job, they had to be measured for the outfits. Betty had designed a green and white outfit for the drinks waitresses, with the shortest of mini skirts. This was the sixties and the Mary Quant style of mini skirts had dispensed the stocking and suspender belt to the dustbin. They had been superseded by tights to avoid the unsightly bit of bare leg. The outfits consisted of a white blouse, green waistcoat with lacing up the front, and a green mini skirt. The food waitresses had the same design but in red and white, with a little starched white pinny to complete the ensemble. Every detail had been taken care of. The outfits looked very smart and were practical; being cotton they were easily laundered. Betty appointed a head waitress. Her name was Peggy. She was responsible for making sure the girls were turned out properly. Any problems, she had to deal with them.

The kitchen was to be staffed by a husband and wife team, Edna and Percy, a couple who had worked for the Corrigans for years. They had the job of cooking all the meals in baskets. Everything was deep fried. The produce was bought in from local suppliers. Will Smithson, the milkman who delivered to Oaks Cottage, got the job of supplying the chicken portions. Close-knit and local was the best way to describe everyone who took part in the operation.

James and Betty poured their very souls into the exciting project. They were by now exhausted and full of self-doubt. They had committed thousands of pounds in signed contracts to forthcoming attractions, three months at an average of £3,000 per week, and that was just for the top of the bill, the tip of the iceberg. When adding on the support acts, wages and all other associated costs, they dare not think of failure, but it had to be at the back of their minds as the last finishing touches were being arrived at.

The time had come. It would soon be clear if their biggest dream would turn into success or failure. Each in their own way had given it their all.

Chapter 4

The Impossible Dream

Overleaf: Queuing to get in on opening night at the Batley Variety Club.

Malcolm Fleming and Tommy Mitchell, two handy men doubling up as bouncers should they have to expel anyone who got out of line, wore the smartest of black evening suits and bow ties and politely helped the first audience through the doors. The lights twinkled, taxis pulled up outside delivering the public to the most glamorous night out ever seen in this old mill town; a town which had been brought to life by the vision of a showman, born and bred to provide entertainment. He knew what people wanted and he was about to deliver.

A large gathering of the press, invited friends and all who had taken part in the build were to witness the event. James and Betty were sitting on the balcony that first night with a few friends. Brother John Edwin and his wife were alongside Auntie Sarah, James's favourite aunt who had invested her lifetime savings into the new venture. They were there to share the great happiness and success this opening night was to bring. The Corrigan family and friends knew how much the couple had ploughed into their latest project. They had to be admired for the courage and fortitude needed to pull off something as big as this. Everyone was over the moon. The club was packed. It was a sell out.

Also there that night was Derek Ford. As James overshot the budget on the building of the club, he approached Derek for an investment, who obliged at a cost and now owned a share of the club. It was not part of Corrigan Ford Enterprises, but a private arrangement between the two. It was a small share but James withheld this fact from Betty. He would of course tell her at the appropriate moment, but this was not the moment. Betty thought Derek was there as an invited guest but, knowing how she felt about him, James did not want to spoil her night. The triumph was as much Betty's as it was James's, for she had designed the club, her concept of an intimate atmosphere had paid off. Not only did it have that, it had soul.

When the lights went down, the band struck up and the first artiste appeared on stage. You felt you could reach out and touch them. The atmosphere was electric, it sent shivers down the spine. The Bachelors performed at their very best, it was nothing short of magic. The show went without a hitch; the audience loved it, the waitresses loved the outfits, they were all part of the show. It was glamour with a capital G. The excitement of it all was palpable. The audience went wild. The stars invited the fans backstage for autographs. They were so pleased with their lounge, they were happy to show it off. The audience was keen to take advantage of the invite and see what was backstage. They certainly liked what they saw at the front and duly lined up to get the inky signatures of the stars on anything that could be written on. Con Clusky, the leader of The Bachelors who had suggested it was below their dignity to perform anywhere other than a theatre, suddenly had changed his mind.

The first show was a huge success, though it has to be said the organisation was little short of pandemonium. Many staff had little or no experience. This was a first for everyone. It was organised chaos. Most of the barmaids had never served drinks before. The place was so big they were losing their customers and spilling drinks, thankfully not over the audience. The food waitresses were no better, food orders were taking forever to arrive at tables, but on the face of it most of the errors were being concealed and all seemed well to the public. The first night's audience was very forgiving of the many delays.

The great gamble had paid off. James Corrigan heaved a sigh of relief. Had all this turned out differently, they would have been completely ruined. Everyone was happy, none more than James, he had achieved the impossible. A first for the north of England; a venue so big there was nothing to touch it. James was the toast of the town.

For anyone who had never heard of Batley, they soon would.

The club was headline news and its success travelled like wildfire. The media could not get enough of this most unlikely of stories. Curiously, the local newspaper *Batley News* was totally underwhelmed. Despite taking a lion's share of the advertising budget every week, they never supported the club. The trade papers though were there in abundance; James Towler, who was the northern reporter for *The Stage* was always in attendance, as was Ron Boyle, the show business correspondent of the *Daily Express*. Any reporters turning up showing their press credentials were treated to a night to remember, they were the bugle blowers of this phenomenon, this phoenix which was rising from the ashes of an industrial wasteland called Batley.

The area was buzzing, the members of Batley Variety Club could not wait for their next big night out. The industrial north was such a depressing place. Gilbert Harding, a social commentator, well known for his radio broadcasts, related being driven into Batley; he described the experience as 'descending into a basin of smoke', the pollution was so bad you could taste the air you breathed. The lines of washing fluttering in the breeze had to be shaken like a rug when taken indoors to expel the soot that poured out of the mill chimneys. Gilbert Harding was not to know that much later the most famous club in the country would be built on a disused sewerage bed amongst all that soot. Imagine what he would have made of that.

In 1967, television was permanently black and white with only two channels: BBC and ITV. Entertainment was broadcast on an evening, four hours after which the national anthem was played. 'God Save the Queen' was succeeded by a white dot which would fade away the picture, usually around 10.30pm. There was no daytime television. Buses full of passengers, travelling on public transport was the norm; if a car was owned, the owner was considered rich! Imagine the Corrigan's showering pot loads of glamour. Wow! It was the biggest story since the end of World War Two.

James was in his element, Batley was even bigger news than the venues in the south, knocking the West End of London off the front pages. James Corrigan was soon becoming as famous as the artistes he was engaging. He was proud of his club but not only that, he was proud of his town, being happy to show it off to the many curious visitors anxious to meet the man who had dreamed up the best good news story to come out of Yorkshire. He was always polite, well spoken and charming, extending a friendly welcome with a cup of tea delivered to his office by Edna, the most endearing cook/friend you could wish to meet. The warmth of welcome was typical of the north.

The first weeks of the club went surprisingly well, given everyone involved was completely without experience. After all, this venture had never been done before. Lighting engineers, door staff, booking office staff, everyone had their jobs to do and as the weeks went on they gained in confidence. What they lacked in experience they made up for in enthusiasm, being eager to be part of the unfolding success.

The club manager was Allan Clegg, as honest as the day was long and full of fun. His appointment was to last for the duration of the club's life. The assistant manager was Gerard Cadden and his wife Eileen was to become the booking office manageress. Lottie, an old retainer from the Victoria Bingo, took charge of the pay desk. Lottie was an amazing woman of advancing years. A tiny lady, she was a character not to be underestimated. She would appear every night before a show opened, taking herself into the pay kiosk, cash box in hand, her face beautifully made-up ready for the serious business of taking the money from the patrons arriving without reservations.

A freelance photographer roamed around taking pictures of the audience. Everyone thought they had fallen into a pot of jam. There were not many jobs around Batley which did not involve being covered in grease, working in a mill, or down a pit hewing out coal. The motto of the West Riding of Yorkshire was 'where there's muck there's brass'. Well that may have been true, but the money was only enough to get from one week to the next. It was a hard-working area and the club was an escape route into a world never known before. What was more, it was for them. They could afford to go and be diverted from the reality of life thanks to the clever mathematics and the ingenious idea which had brought this about. It was special. Special enough to get the tin bath off the wall and get suited and booted.

The people of the north were not about to let the side down. If all these top stars were in town, they wanted them to know that the typical image of whippets and flat caps was a myth. They had, at last, a reason to get dressed up and go out and celebrate. Any event, anniversaries, birthdays were noted and celebrated. Flowers would be sent to the club for an unsuspecting member of the audience, who would be invited on stage to receive a special presentation, often by the artistes. The ladies had shed the mill pinnies and hair curlers for long dresses; they turned up walking tall. James Corrigan stood on the balcony watching them take their seats. He was so moved to see the transformation which had taken place, he was very proud of them. Yes it was a business venture, but to witness this change in people was nothing less than to see a piece of social engineering.

He had changed the landscape of Batley, breathing happiness and joy into a long-neglected town. The waitresses were walking on air, for although their wages were not a fortune, they got tips, some as much as ten shillings a night. They went home skipping down the road. When everything had settled down, a van was bought to take the girls home after the shows. Sometimes it would be as late as one o'clock in the morning when they finished work and James and Betty needed to know they were home safely.

James found room for three young local ladies who had formed a dance troupe called 'The Deb Set'. They were very young and eager to please. James gave them a filling-in slot between acts and after their first run James went to see them to politely say that he appreciated all their hard work, but perhaps the Variety Club wasn't the stage for them. When he walked in the room, he saw the girls beavering away at making their own costumes. James was so impressed with their enthusiasm he had a change of heart and told them that not only could they continue to work at the club, but that they should be employed directly, thus making sure they did not have to pay the agent's commission.

From the opening week onwards, artistes were lined up to carry on the run of top names. One followed another at £3,000 for a week's appearance. To keep the momentum going, James soon cast his net further than the London agents and approached the rich vein of talent in America. It was Dean Martin he had his heart set on. When the Corrigan family went for a drive out on a Sunday afternoon, Dean Martin's hit songs blared from the tape cassette. James, Jamie and Betty would sing along knowing all the words off by heart. He was by far their favourite of all the American singers around at the time. He had good looks, charm and a very easy style. The best of the crooners in their opinion. James was not a bad judge when it came to knowing what audiences wanted and it was his job to deliver up the best money could buy. As far as he was concerned, this had become his new role in life.

Bernard Hinchcliffe and James went to America with a shopping list, at the top of which was Dean Martin. A meeting was set up with his manager. James and Bernard approached the offices smartly turned out, looking the part of Englishmen with money. They were a little nervous but determined not to let it show. James entered the plush office with his usual aplomb, seated was Dean's manager. They shook hands and sat down to discuss the prospect of engaging Dean Martin and bringing him to Batley. James explained how he had built the north of England's biggest nightclub and related all the advantages of a week's stay in Batley.

The manager got a map out of his drawer to help James explain where on the map this little town was. To James's embarrassment, he could not find Batley. Bernard sat back watching James smooth talk his way into the subject of a fee. By this time Dean Martin's manager was looking unconvinced but James was not to be fazed by the lack of enthusiasm he was encountering and ploughed on. He offered a figure which was larger than he had offered anyone else: £45,000. When he did so, he offered a prayer to God at the same time. This was an astronomical amount; one which he knew would be stretching his finances to the very limit.

Dean's manager choked on his cigar and said, 'My boy would not get out of bed to piss for that amount.' On reflection, he may have done James a great favour. To recover that amount of money was maybe a step too far.

Feeling deeply embarrassed, James departed with his tail between his legs. But when Bernard and James left the office, they doubled up laughing at the reaction they'd got. James was a fun-loving man with a wonderful smile and the warmest heart. He could cope with any put down, no matter who delivered it.

Not to be defeated, they carried on with their quest for big-name artistes. The trip to America was not a complete waste of time; whilst there, the two men visited the theatrical agencies and left calling cards. Most of the recipients had never heard of Yorkshire, let alone Batley. It was impossible to find on a map as they had earlier discovered. They went into the office of Joe Glaser, president of Associated Booking Corporation, ABC for short, whose office was on Park Avenue, New York. Joe Glaser's organisation handled an extensive list of artistes, to put it mildly. His roster of stars included Barbra Streisand, Noel Coward, Louis Armstrong, Billie Holiday and Duke Ellington to name a few. It was Louis Armstrong that James had his sights set on. To bring the great Satchmo to England would be the biggest coup of all. Imagine the publicity it would generate.

James and Bernard had to talk long and hard with Joe Glaser, who had a reputation of being a bit of a hoodlum in his early days. After much negotiating, a deal was struck. Louis Armstrong was to appear at Batley with his All Stars band at huge expense to James, for not only was he paying a handsome fee but he was footing the bill for the first-class travelling expenses of the entire entourage. The figure which was eventually arrived at should have remained a secret, alas, to the eternal regret of James, he told the press the £27,000 fee, believing it was part of the story. With this revelation came his first big mistake; it signalled to the agents and managers of the showbiz world that Batley was a pot of gold. Any future negotiations would start with the telephone figures paid to Satchmo uppermost in their minds and, although there was only one Louis Armstrong, it was abundantly clear to all that the pockets of Batley were very deep indeed.

The club was beginning to settle down and started to run like a well-oiled machine. The staff had now got to grips with the routine; the waitresses had stopped spilling drinks and knew how to bob with a tray whilst avoiding showing their underwear.

James had to break down the snobbery of the London managements, and to convince them their artists would be well looked after. The Variety Club was not yet established as a venue of great note and when their artistes had climbed to the top of the ladder, they wanted the prestigious bookings as a mark of their success. Television was the most powerful vehicle of all to enhance the reputation of any artiste. After this was the Grade /Delfont organisation. These people controlled the business, having theatres in the West End of London, the Palladium being the top venue, playing host to Royal Command Performances over the years.

James was not to be deterred by the show-business moguls jealously guarding their reputations of being the best. He challenged all this nonsense. This task was helped greatly by the artistes themselves; once they had come north and found the warmth of the welcome and enjoyed the facilities, they could not wait to tell their friends in the business what a wonderful time they had working the date. James and the staff made everyone welcome, there was no star-struck adoration. After all they were no different to the rest of us, they had been fortunate enough to possess a talent, which when exploited would lead them through a gentler way of life than the rest of us. They were there to do a job. Whilst respected, they were not revered or worshipped. The artistes loved the down to earth approach, the family atmosphere of the place. They felt like kings, loving the closeness of the audience, something they had never experienced in other types of venues.

The club routine was the same week after week. The closure of the Saturday night show marked the end of a week. Sunday brought a change in the bill and a new show. The incoming artistes, their entourage, road managers etc, descended around lunchtime, ready to start rehearsals for the week's engagement. It was action stations. The billing displayed outside the club had to be changed, technicians sprang into action, working out the lighting plots for the different acts. The control room boys, in charge of the sound and lights, were on top of their game. Keith Davies and Brian Dewhirst becoming excellent technicians. All in all James was a lucky man. Although he had a small team around him to turn his dream into a reality, everyone stepped up to the plate. The success was a collective achievement.

Usually four supporting acts, plus the top of the bill, would be the ideal line-up for a show. The musicians were on stage, ready to accompany singers or to play the acts on and play them off at the end of their performance. It was a hive of theatrical activity. The kitchen was on standby supplying all the tea and coffee needed to keep everyone going. It seemed at times like musical mayhem. The rehearsals usually ended an hour before the club was due to open, giving the staff and musicians enough time to get home and ready for the opening night of the show. When everyone was happy, a running order was worked out, typed and pinned up backstage to let the stage manager know what time each performer was to be on stage.

The artistes were very pleasantly surprised when they found complementary drinks waiting for them in the well-appointed dressing rooms. Hospitality was not in short supply for the visiting entertainers, they loved the homespun welcome and charm of the owner and management, who could not do enough to make their stay as pleasant an experience as possible.

Oaks Cottage had by now been transformed by Betty; they had a beautiful home, immaculately furnished with no expense spared in the process. The kitchen was fitted out with the latest gadgets, it was truly a dream home. James had, over the years, collected antique armour and weapons and the local antique dealer, Leon Cooper, was a constant visitor, selling his latest finds, usually old guns and swords, which Betty tastefully arranged on the walls.

One day Leon came rushing in excited to have found a table which was reputed to be a betrothal present from Philip II of Spain to Elizabeth I of England. James and Betty took off to see the rare find. The table was a huge piece of furniture made of dark oak wood, carved with the heraldic emblems of Spain and England. We all know Elizabeth never married, but Philip did propose to her and the offer was eventually turned down. The table came with provenance supporting its pedigree. They bought it at great expense and gave it pride of place in their home. It was a wonderful talking point and particularly interesting to the American artistes who, over the years, would stay with them. Needless to say it was a show piece. And never to be used.

Betty was to turn one room of the house into an office and study for James. All the confidential dealings could take place there, rather than at the club where the constant comings and goings were distracting and made it impossible to work. It seemed anyone and everyone wanted to meet James and pat him on the back. He had become the people's champion. He had a talent for making anyone he spoke to feel special, always polite and entirely interested in all they said. He could have been bored stiff by the tales he was told but the narrators would never know, he had patience in abundance. On numerous occasions people would claim to be a friend of 'Jimmy Corrigan'. That was to give lie to the statement as James hated being called Jimmy, any friend of his knew better; he was always James to his close friends.

Their home, which had started out as a modest little shell, had now grown into a thirteen-room hacienda sitting in landscaped gardens with a stream running through, carefully tended by a full-time gardener. Later, Betty was to put the full stop on the project by building the most beautiful indoor swimming pool with changing rooms and a bar. One wall was made up of French windows with toffee-coloured glass, specially made to her design. When sunlight shone, a honey glow was thrown across the shimmering blue water, acting like an enormous pair of sunglasses. Betty's initials were incorporated on the floor of the pool in a mosaic of blue tiles, her signature on the masterpiece which she had created.

There was nothing to touch the luxury of Oaks Cottage. It was a home fit for a queen and, make no mistake, the queen was Betty. If James was becoming the 'King of Clubs', Betty was to be the 'Queen of Diamonds'. She could not get enough of them, or fur coats. They were both to acquire the trappings of the rich and famous. James was the one who had become famous, basking in the limelight the world's press chose to shine on him. He was happy to take credit for the finest venue in the country, taking variety to a new dimension.

Variety had been around for generations, but the music halls had moved to the theatres and the theatres were closing. James Corrigan had dreamed up the latest concept for entertaining the people. He was to be the pioneer of the nightclub. Betty played a large part but, unlike James, she was not one for the limelight and stepped back, allowing her husband to claim all the credit despite the fact they had both put their all into it. Happily it was a gamble which paid off and not just for the Corrigans, the whole area and the people in it were the beneficiaries.

Chapter 5

Who Can I Turn To?

Overleaf: Pauline and me.

Betty discovered she was pregnant with a second child. Con Clusky's wife was pregnant at the same time, and the two families became great friends, spending lots of time together.

Betty gave birth to a little baby boy and named him Jason. Jamie, who was now fourteen, was thrilled to have a new baby brother. It was Sally, Betty's mother, who took control of Jason. Sally, a widow, was a dear sweet lady who had worked hard all her life and was now seeing her daughter enjoy the luxuries which had been denied her. Sally was happy to take charge of her two grandsons, leaving Betty free to run the bingo and make sure everything was going well with the club. Whilst the children had the warmth and love of their grandma, they had less of the same from their mother who was becoming increasingly remote from their lives. Everything seemed to take precedence over them. She had an army of cleaners at Oaks Cottage and if Grandma was not around, the cleaners became a substitute for the children's attention.

Betty had an unnerving effect on the staff. James could get what he wanted by oozing charm, whereas Betty had no winning ways. Instead, she instilled the fear of God into them. It was a classic case of 'good cop, bad cop'. This led to a split camp; one side with James, the other Betty. Deep down, Betty was much kinder than she allowed anyone to see. Unfortunately, not many people were allowed to get close enough to discover this.

Betty talked the Cluskys into moving north. They discovered the many beauty spots on the outskirts of towns that opened up on to the Yorkshire Dales, where the rolling hills and the most spectacular countryside could be reached by driving eight miles in any direction. Waterfalls sparkled down rocky crags, rivers and streams meandered through the most beautiful county in the world. God's own county.

With Betty's help, the Cluskys found an old manor house on the outskirts of Elland, a satellite of Halifax. It was a wonderful find, set in its own grounds and enjoyed total seclusion, a must for the famous singer who was going to live there. It had a minstrels' gallery, which was an unusual feature in a house and became a talking point. It made for an ideal family home for the Cluskys' growing family.

The M1 brought London into commuting distance with the north. The heart of London could be reached in three hours. The Bachelors were managed by a London agency and often had to be there. The act was in huge demand and were being kept busy by their many appearances all over the country. After the Cluskys bought the house, Betty lent her support and expertise in having it renovated. She was more than willing to help make their dream home a reality, during which time the two families came together under the roof of the Corrigans; the Cluskys staying as guests while the major work and renovation was carried out on their new home in Elland. Whether by design or accident, Betty was becoming deeply attracted to Con. They became very close and a relationship ensued.

Shortly after the club opened, James had been caught up in an argument over a front row table which had been double booked. A most attractive young lady had booked the table for herself and her mother, only to find someone in their seats when they arrived. She was in a high state of agitation and demanded to see the manager. James went down to sort out the problem. Not knowing who he was, she was abusive. To avoid a scene, he introduced himself and invited her and her mother to see the show from the balcony. He escorted them up to the very special area, ordered champagne and treated them with the utmost courtesy. They were over the moon, watching the show from this privileged position. When it was time to leave, James offered to run them home in his grey Barracuda car. But this isn't the end of the story. James quickly became besotted and a clandestine relationship ensued.

The young lady's name was Pauline and she worked as a manager of a dress shop in neighbouring Dewsbury. She was a marvellous advert for the fashion trade, wearing the latest designs to great effect. She was only 20, a blonde beauty with a figure to die for, a bubbly personality and an outsize sense of humour. James was in his early forties, but he was not going to let a little thing like that stand in his way. He made a date with her and, surprisingly, her mother was to approve. Maybe the champagne had gone to her head.

Around the time that Pauline first met James, she was to make a new friend: myself, Maureen Prest. I was having some matrimonial troubles of my own at the time and we compared notes. I tried to solve Pauline's dilemma; she had fallen in love with a married man. Pauline acted as my wailing wall because I had fallen out of love having discovered my husband was having an affair. As one of his many mistresses pointed out to me one day over the telephone, 'It wasn't a hand-holding affair.'

James was showering Pauline with gifts galore, indulging her in anything she wanted. I had bred a litter of puppies from my white toy poodle named Wendy. They were very cute little things and when Pauline saw them she wanted one. She dragged James along to see the fluffy balls of cuteness and he bought a puppy which Pauline named Skippy. They were captivated by the new little dog, Very soon we three became friends.

The weeks which followed were a whirlwind of business meetings for James, punctuated by stealing time away from the office to see Pauline. They were like two love birds; he was head over heels. He pulled up at her house shortly after they met in a gleaming brand new Rolls Royce. He tooted his horn, beckoned her to jump in, and took her for a drive in his latest acquisition. It was a wonderful car in royal blue with ivory leather, the seats were piped with the same colour as the body of the car, the leather was sumptuous and smelled gorgeous, the walnut veneer was polished to perfection. It glided off as smooth as treacle with Dean Martin blaring out of the 8-track stereo. This was James's ultimate status symbol. The car turned heads as it travelled around the local towns. There was only one man who could afford such a rare and beautiful vehicle. James had arrived and everyone knew it.

On one occasion, James took Pauline to London where he had a meeting with Lord Lew Grade, the great impresario and head of the famous Grade Organisation who were agents to the top stars in show business. They were wined and dined at a high-class hotel. Lew Grade was charmed by Pauline and asked her to try the smoked salmon. Being young and naïve and never having tasted it before, she agreed. When the smoked salmon arrived she thought, 'Fucking hell, they eat raw fish in London!' Fortunately she was polite enough not to air her true feelings.

Another time there was a trip to Scarborough. James had bought a boat; it was a cruiser with accommodation for six people. He took a couple of the staff from the club as crew to sail the craft on a maiden voyage from Scarborough to Bridlington. The plan was to stay on board overnight and to make the trip down the coast on the early tide. Pauline, not being keen on sailing, had arranged that she be offloaded before they left, preferring to drive the car and meet the crew on arrival in port.

They slept on board overnight and when Pauline awoke they were already en route. She opened her eyes to the rolling of the boat and could feel herself being tossed about on the North Sea like a cork. She became hysterical, grabbed the first thing to hand, a torch, and started beating James about the head with it. She was absolutely terrified of the sea and couldn't believe they had all betrayed her trust. To say she was a reluctant passenger was an understatement. By the time they got to Bridlington, James had a very sore head and a sore stomach with the laughter at her reaction to the trip.

James and Betty were not to know that they had both cast their nets outside their marriage, both deceiving each other. The tangled web they both wove was to bring great unhappiness, not only to themselves but to lots of other people who were caught up in their deceptions. The staff were extra careful not to let any cats out of the bags; none of them wished to be disloyal and they were fearful of losing their positions. It was a situation which made everyone very uncomfortable. The Corrigans were to be the biggest losers though, it was just a question of time before the bubble would burst.

I was experiencing the most traumatic of times. I had two young sons, Nigel and Chris, and was constantly soul searching, trying to work out what was best for all concerned. Eventually I gained a divorce, taking myself and the children away to start a new life alone. I had turned my back on the security of a comfortable home and a family business to embark upon a new life. Uprooting my children and taking them to this stark new existence was not a decision I took lightly. My husband may have had the morals of an alley cat but he had been pretty good as a father. Nigel was eight, Chris was five. It was hard taking a leap into the unknown. Although a court had made financial provision for the children from the father, there was no guarantee he would honour the terms.

Finding a suitable flat in Dewsbury, I took my boys and moved in with the minimum of belongings. We had no luxuries, we didn't even have a carpet on the floor. Pauline was with me the day we moved and had been a constant support. As she viewed what little I had, she said I was mad leaving everything behind. 'If this had been me I would have taken the paper off the walls.' But I wanted no reminders of the life I was leaving behind.

Christmas was around the corner and I had very little money. I saw a wanted ad for a driver to deliver groceries for a local shop. I got the job, driving a Ford Transit van, a monster of a thing, the gears crunching with years of abuse from former drivers. I had to carry huge cardboard boxes of groceries to the shoppers of the town. It was the winter of 1967, my only ambition was to buy two Timex watches for my sons as Christmas presents and to provide them with a decent Christmas after the trauma of the move. I was slipping and sliding up and down garden paths.

It was freezing cold and I was wrapped up like Nanook of the North for the minimum of pay.

During these dark days I was morally supported by James and Pauline. They were so kind. I was twenty-six, a woman of principle. It was not often divorce was a solution to a failing marriage in 1967. One could only be obtained on the grounds of adultery; I certainly had those. Using this as the exit, I was to win my freedom, blazing the trail for others to follow. Times were changing, people were no longer staying together 'for the sake of the children' in a loveless marriage.

The Transit van was forever breaking down. It was a battered wreck, previous drivers having bumped every corner. Not being fazed, I soldiered on and arrived at Christmas with enough money to buy my two sons the coveted watches, food for the holiday and ten pounds to spare. The money was placed in a cigarette box to tide us over until the next pay day. I invited a few friends to share a drink and nibbles in my new home, sparse though it was. When the guests had left, I went to take the ten pound note out of the box and found it was gone! One of my so-called friends had helped themselves to the last of our money. I was devastated. Now we were penniless.

Not to be deflated, I carried on with the driving job. One day I called in at the club and when James spotted me driving the battered van he asked me into his office. He ordered tea from Edna in the kitchen and she came up with a tray of tea and toast. After a friendly chat, completely out of the blue James said, 'I have been thinking. We have had a long run of top-named artistes but there are not enough of them to fill the club fifty-two weeks a year, so we are now having to book the second division. I know they won't fill the place but, with your help, I have thought of a plan!' I was a very capable businesswoman before the domestic split and I was interested to hear what he was to propose.

He offered me the job of Promotions Manager for the club. We chatted it through, both throwing in ideas as to how we could fill the place. He had the idea to give out free tickets but it was to be kept very hush-hush. He did not want the future artistes to know the place was being 'papered'. As a front for the job, I would be the ambassador representing the club in any way I could to promote it in the public eye, deal with the many reporters' questions and send out the many press releases relating to the future artistes' appearances. After reaching an agreement, I took the job. It didn't take long to decide! He told me to take that battered van back to base and tell them to put it where the sun did not shine.

My life was to change dramatically. I was now able to provide more than we had before making my bid for freedom. My guilt towards my children was to disappear. After feeling uncomfortable that I had plucked them from the matrimonial home, I could now start to rebuild our lives with the security of a well-paid job.

It was a job which I took very seriously, I gave it my all in terms of thought and energy. I was to become the Variety Club's best kept secret. James was delighted with the outcome. I never betrayed the confidence he placed in my skills as a hard-working public relations officer. He let me get on with the job, leaving it to my judgement as to how I developed the role. I put more bums on seats than any of the artistes.

Just as James was a people's person, so was I. My first thought was to single out workplaces in the community where the workers would be most grateful of a cheap night out. I targeted the hospitals; the nurses and hospital staff welcomed the special consideration. I went to Leeds General Infirmary and saw the head porter, who was a very active organiser of all things social, not just for the staff but also the patients. He was so happy to see me. He took me into his office and we chatted over a coffee. He used an empty lecture room every Wednesday to put on a show for the patients who were able to get out of bed and take a trip to see the artistes who were appearing in the local working men's clubs and who had volunteered to perform for the poorly folks of Leeds. They had a sound engineer on hand to record the event which was then broadcast throughout the hospital; usually by someone from Radio Leeds. He explained how he thought it helped patients get better quicker; they often had a comedian to make the patients laugh, distracting them from their illness, if only for an hour, believing 'laughter was the best medicine'. I had to agree.

Not only was the porter prepared to dole out the tickets for our shows, he asked if I would mind bringing some artistes who could take part in the Wednesday concert. Thinking about it, I could see how the Variety Club would benefit by engaging in the operation. I could approach the support acts, though not the top of the bill artistes, their contracts had a watertight clause which prevented them from appearing elsewhere for the duration of the contract. The support acts were at a loose end during the day and they jumped at the opportunity to join me. I took them on the eight-mile journey and we were made to feel like royalty walking into the hospital. The patients were so grateful for the chance to have first-class entertainment. They loved meeting the artistes and the hospital was abuzz as the patients got back to the wards, telling the bed-bound patients all about the lunchtime show. It gave them something different to talk about other than their ailments. Afterwards, the artiste did an interview with Radio Leeds, plugging the club and promoting themselves in the process.

I was to make Wednesdays my reality check day, it kept my feet firmly on the ground and in touch with the reality of life. The club was a world of make believe, far removed from the work-a-day existence I was familiar with. Money was talked about in telephone numbers and I was afraid of losing all sense of proportion. I welcomed any diversion away from these new circumstances. Being with the workers of the area kept me well and truly grounded. It became a special day for me and one which I looked forward to. As far as I could see it was all a question of balance.

Shortly after I started working at the club, Bob Monkhouse was to appear. We got a letter from a young man who had been in hospital all his life and for a time had been with Bob's son,

Gary, who also suffered from the same illness. He was wheelchair bound and not able to feed himself nor drink without assistance. I asked Mr Monkhouse if he would be willing to see the young man if I arranged a visit whilst he was appearing at the club. He was delighted to oblige. Come the due date, the young man in question was brought to the club to meet his hero. The press declined to attend on the grounds the story would offend public opinion! How disgraceful. What would that young man have felt if he had known his appearance was deemed too unsavoury for a newspaper? Mercifully, he did not know and he enjoyed meeting up with his pal's dad.

Shortly after Bob Monkhouse left, Des O'Connor came along. He stayed with James and Betty. Des was a lovely man, a joy to be around, always telling funny stories. He had a passion for the horses and spent his afternoons studying form and placing bets with his bookmaker in London. The club was doing good business and everybody was happy. It was a good week except that after he left, James got the most expensive telephone bill ever, thanks to Des making long distance calls to his bookmaker in London.

Chapter 6

What A Wonderful World

Overleaf: James, Louis Armstrong and Betty.

The bingo business was going from strength to strength. With new halls being opened on a regular basis, the Corrigan Ford Enterprises knew no bounds. However, with such financial success comes envy. James had his imitators.

There was a company known by the name of Bartle Enterprises who owned a few bingo halls. Colin Bartle was the head of the company; a tall, fair-haired man, well dressed with a commanding presence. He wore rimless glasses and a camel overcoat, and looked the part of a successful businessman. He was a thorn in James's side, trying to emulate him every step of the way; if James opened a bingo hall you could bet within a short space of time Colin Bartle would open one within a few miles of him. The rivalry was huge, both men trying to outdo each other, but Bartle was a small-time player compared to James. He was mirroring his success. The club was no different.

Bartle watched the success of the Variety Club unfold. This clearly was the next big thing, with crowds flocking every night of the week to be entertained. Bartle leased some land in the neighbouring town of Wakefield which belonged to Wakefield Trinity rugby league club. Mr Bartle decided to build a theatre club, it was to be much more luxurious than Batley. He used the same building company and no doubt picked the brains of the builders. They used the same format of the Batley club, enhancing it enough for them to claim it was superior. It would seem James Corrigan was not going to have it all his own way.

When James discovered what was happening, he put the word out around the agents in London; if any of their artistes worked for the Wakefield club, they would not be working for his. James did everything in his power to scupper the plans of the competition. He made it very hard for them to secure any artistes, certainly of note. Anything James could do to sabotage the planned venue was done. James Corrigan was a crafty man. Not only did he spell out to the agents his terms and conditions, he had the artistes staying at his now luxurious home. He figured having made friends under his roof, he could rely on their loyalty to him, preventing them from working for the competition. James always had an ulterior motive and, when he turned on the charm offensive, he was a force to be reckoned with.

Shortly after the Wakefield club opened, James took the club photographer to one side, telling him to go to Wakefield and get the job of taking photographs of the audiences. He offered him the concession in Batley for free, provided he came back every night and reported to him how the business was going in the opposition's club. Naturally the photographer jumped at the chance. He got the job, was James's spy and in turn had the run of Batley free. It was a pot of gold and James had a daily report of how Bartle's new business was running.

James would also send a driver out to count the number of cars in the car park, always a good sign of how well the place was doing. The reports pleased him; it was struggling from day one. All the negative reports put a spring in the step of the Batley Variety Club owner. He had stolen a march on the rival club; despite the superior building which Wakefield enjoyed, it did not have the soul.

Bartle wasn't averse to fighting back, though. One night in 1968, Georgie Fame was appearing at Batley. Just as he went on stage, dozens of policemen marched into the club. Georgie was sat at the piano. He saw what was happening and started playing the theme tune from *Z Cars*, a popular police drama on TV at that time. The audience thought it was hilarious. When the management looked out on to the road, they saw a fleet of police vans carrying a police army. The management asked what was happening. It seemed the club had been reported for admitting non-members. The timing of the raid was strategically timed to take place after the normal closing hours of the licensed trade, 11pm. The top of the bill normally arrived on stage at 11pm. Technically, before that time no one could be accused of committing an offence. The audience had to stay seated and no one was allowed to leave until all membership cards had been checked. It would seem after all the checks and double checks nothing was amiss, so no charges were brought. Who could have been the complainant? Could it have been the very bitter Mr Colin Bartle?

Later the government relaxed the licensing law and any premises serving food and drink could apply for a supper license. Once granted they could overcome the closing times. This was a great relief to Batley. As food was already served at the club, a license was sought and granted, thus avoiding the tedium of the membership cards. Anyone could now be admitted, member or not.

Jayne Mansfield, the blonde sex-bombshell, was coming to England and her management was booking her in cabaret. No one had seen her act but her name was enough to generate interest. James chased her down to The Scotch Corner Hotel near Catterick in North Yorkshire thinking that he could lure her to Batley by offering her a week at his club. She could stay in his beautiful home, away from the crowds. He knocked on her door and entered. There were three or four tiny Chihuahuas running all over the place. She had smuggled them into the country under the fur coat she placed over her arm as she stepped down off the plane on arrival in England, thus avoiding the quarantine laws. The room was a mess, the dogs had shit everywhere. The smell was appalling. Instead of cleaning it up, she and her boyfriend placed newspapers over the mess and paper was dotted all over the room. They carried on walking over it. When James saw this, he dropped the idea of offering her his hospitality at Oaks Cottage, Betty would have had a fit had she seen the mess. He talked her into doing a week at the club and suggested she stay at the Queens Hotel in Leeds.

Naturally, ever the showman, James set the publicity in motion. When she arrived she was given a civic reception and signed the visitor's book in the mayor's parlour in Batley Town

Hall. Later she was to meet the national press in James's office at the club, where they anxiously awaited the arrival of the great Miss Mansfield. The photographers could not get enough of her. She did not disappoint, her bosoms were falling out of her tight-fitting dress. They took pictures of every angle. She was even asked to lay across James's desk. She said that as she did not wear underwear, it may be difficult trying to achieve that angle without revealing her private bits! TV cameras were there, the publicity was huge.

When she opened on the Sunday night, everyone was wondering what she would do. Was she a singer? The curtain went back and there she stood, sex bomb extraordinaire, and started to recite Shakespeare! Well, strangely, the Batley audiences were not switched on by a Tudor poet. After ten minutes they started walking out.

James was mortified. He was a man of the people and his club was for them. His aim was to please his audiences; to have them leave whilst the show was in progress was a situation he had to rectify as soon as possible.

When the show was over he had words with Miss Mansfield, explaining, as tactfully as he possibly could, that she should play to her strengths. I think he meant flaunt herself. Do anything but don't recite poetry. The following night she duly complied with the wishes of the management and walked amongst the audience sitting on the men's laps. They were getting all hot under the collar; this Hollywood legend was in their midst flirting with the population of Yorkshire. To be truthful, she did not have an act, just a name. Sadly, shortly after leaving Batley and returning home to her native America, she was killed in a car crash.

When Yorkshire Television studios opened in Leeds, the management entered into negotiations with James. They had the idea of using Batley Variety Club as a northern version of *Sunday Night at the London Palladium*. They talked James into doing a pilot film at the club. It was more a feasibility study into how the technical difficulties of staging a show for television could be overcome; working out lighting plots and sound effects for the medium of television. They would put their own act in for a segment of the show. Reluctantly, James agreed and gave them the run of the place.

The day duly arrived and people from the studios were soon crawling all over. Being a new station, the technicians were new to the job but, despite this, they thought they were God's gift to entertainment, supposing that being in television set them apart from mere mortals. They got up everyone's nose. Cables and wires were everywhere. People were tripping over them.

They were to make their pilot in the interval, between the acts of the Batley schedule. They brought a double act by the name of Hope and Keen. It was pretty third rate compared to the high standards of Batley. James was assured though that their show would never be seen. He most certainly did not want the lacklustre performance he had witnessed put forward as a sample of what could be expected at his club. By the time the technicians had packed their things and gone, everyone heaved a sigh of relief, as did the audience. They had caused much disruption to the place. It was impossible to see how such a show could be produced; no one was impressed. There were so many misgivings it was doubtful they would make another outdoor broadcast from there again.

Yorkshire Television had not fully opened at the time of this incident but they were in preparation, gathering as much material as possible. The day of the first broadcast by the new station brought with it trouble. The technicians went on strike for more pay. Despite giving James assurances that the pilot they had filmed would never be broadcast, in desperation the show went out, as did everything else Yorkshire Television had in the cans.

James hit the roof when he saw the pathetic show which had been filmed. He had spent a fortune getting the right format and artists for his venue and for it to be portrayed in this way was to him the biggest insult of all time. It was broadcast throughout the region, taking in Humberside and Lincolnshire and not just Yorkshire. James fell out with Yorkshire Television and they were not allowed through the doors after this incident. He wanted nothing more to do with them. He now had his work cut out repairing the damage they had done. Fortunately for James, the Louis Armstrong show was nearing its appearance date.

Louis Armstrong and His All Stars landed at Leeds airport and were greeted by a battery of press. A musical family from Leeds was there to meet the living legend. The youngest, a boy by the name of Enrico Tomasso, was allowed onto the tarmac to blow his trumpet for the great man as he stepped down from the plane. Louis looked around to see this little tot of a boy welcoming him to Yorkshire by blowing his trumpet. Louis was delighted. He reached down to shake his hand and invited him to the club to learn the instrument by watching him on stage every night. Louis never had any children of his own, and Little Enrico became the apple of his eye.

When James drove to Leeds to collect him for the first show, there was a crowd of people gathered outside the door of the Queens Hotel. They were there to catch a glimpse of the great Louis Armstrong. He was delighted to see them all and took the opportunity of chatting with them. He was in no rush to get away, delighting in their company. When his manager reminded him that they should go, he said to him, 'These are my people, I am not to be hurried.' He was from a very poor background and had not been to school. A little black boy from the Deep South of America, in his day, was not afforded an education. His talent was to be his escape route out of that world of prejudice.

He was the greatest jazz musician of all time and had just made it to the top of the charts with the song 'What A Wonderful World'. The man was a genius and so humble. After the shows, the fans lined up to get his autograph and I sat by his side telling him how to spell their names as he wanted to make the signings personal. He loved people.

Louis Armstrong had been a giant of a man but when he arrived in Batley he had shed stones of weight and was a shadow of his former self. He had been on a diet which involved a herb called 'Swiss Kriss'. This was infused in hot water and drunk. The only food to be eaten was fruit. The message had been sent in advance that he had to have a daily supply of fresh fruit in his dressing room.

He had copies of his diet printed out to give to anyone who was interested in losing weight, with a little sachet of the herb stapled to the corner of each sheet of paper. He had the staff taking drinks of his Swiss Kriss, then sat back and waited for the result. He had 'forgotten' to make it clear the herb was the strongest laxative ever. The result was dramatic. All the toilets were soon engaged. The great Satchmo thought it was hilarious.

The show was booked for two weeks. The publicity was tremendous and people were coming from all over the country to see his show. They were not disappointed, he gave it his all. He loved Batley and the people loved him.

One night, a member of Louis's entourage was sat talking to James in his office, sharing a joke, when suddenly he had a heart attack. Frantic efforts were made to revive him, all to no avail. The doctor was called but it was too late. Louis Armstrong was on stage, performing to the capacity audience, unaware of the drama that was unfolding in James's office.

Poor Louis was devastated by the loss of his friend. James was devastated at seeing someone perfectly well one minute and gone the next. His body was removed and, as with all sudden deaths, a post-mortem examination was performed to determine the cause of death. Shortly afterwards, his remains were flown home to his family in America. The public never knew of the tragedy. 'The show must go on' is the motto of show business.

Despite the many difficulties, Louis Armstrong and His All Stars was a huge success. James lost money on it but what he lost in financial terms, he more than made up for in publicity. The amount of exposure the club gained due to that appearance could not have been bought. By now everyone knew where Batley in Yorkshire was, never again would James struggle to point it out on the map. The town was famous, eclipsing the West End of London for the brightest stars to appear in this country.

The fee paid in 1968 was £27,000 plus expenses. That sum translates into today's values as nearly half a million pounds, a huge sum. It was to start an escalation of fees being asked by the artistes and managements. James eternally regretted having revealed the fee he paid for the Louis Armstrong show. He was unknowingly putting a noose around his neck.

Just like Louis Armstrong, James loved his practical jokes; he would go to the car park and pretend to be the car park attendant, borrowing the cap and coat from the real attendant. He pulled the cap down low over his face and when the artistes arrived he would show them to their space asking them if there was anything he could do to help them. They would give him a tip, unaware they had just met the owner of the club.

When Shirley Bassey was due to appear at the club for the first time, James discovered she liked Mars bars. He sent one of the staff to the local cash and carry where he bought boxes and boxes of them and stacked them up in her dressing room, ready for her arrival. She thought it was a huge joke, she had enough Mars bars to last a lifetime. She later was to recall how, after that, she could not look a Mars bar in the face again.

James and the club manager Allan Clegg invited Shirley out after a show for a meal. She gratefully accepted, got herself ready, put on her mink jacket and looked for all the world the star she was. They set off in the Rolls Royce, pulling up outside the local fish and chip shop. She thought it was hilarious, having her supper eating fish and chips out of the paper they were wrapped in. Although she was most entertained by the experience, Miss Bassey did live up to her reputation as a diva. She had the most demands of any artiste ever to appear at Batley. There were to be no bars open, or food served whilst she performed. She had to have special hooks fitted in her dressing room to take her many fabulous costumes, all with long trains, sequins and feathers.

She was a very temperamental artist to say the least. The musicians were shaking in their shoes at her band call. When she wanted them to stop playing, her fingers went into her mouth and she gave a high-pitched whistle. Most unladylike. The swear words she used were usually reserved only for a trooper. That said, she was a true perfectionist.

The first time she appeared at Batley she had engaged the services of a new musical director, Brian Fahey, who had not worked with her before. He had accepted the job reluctantly, knowing of her reputation for being difficult to please. When her manager had rung him asking if he would work with her for the duration of the date at Batley, he quoted a ridiculously high figure, hoping the fee would be too much. Alas, to his regret, they assured him that his fee was acceptable. He knew he would be in for a rough ride. He was not wrong. After the first performance, Miss Bassey was less than happy, grumbling about this and that, the musical notation was all wrong and so on, despite the fact she had brought her audience to their feet and they refused to let her leave the stage.

In desperation, Brian gathered up all the music and went into her dressing room. He sat down and assured her he wanted her to be happy with the musical backing and therefore thought it would be a good idea to go through the music note by note. As this was the first time they had worked together, it was important to him that she should feel comfortable. All he wanted was to make sure she was happy. He meticulously went through every band part asking her at regular intervals if she was okay with the music. She assured him she was. Eventually they arrived at the end, changing nothing. From that day forward, Brian and Shirley Bassey got on like a house on fire and he remained with her for many years.

James was worried by the non-sale of drinks and food she had stipulated. He was paying a large sum for the week and needed the revenue to foot the bill. It was announced before she was due to appear on stage that the bars would be closed. James need not have worried. The audience knowing this, ordered lines of drinks before she went on stage. In fact it was later revealed they sold more drinks not less; the audience were not to be denied their booze and over-ordered.

Shirley Bassey was, and is, the greatest star this country has ever produced. She gave the performance of her life on her opening night. She made the most dramatic of entrances, arms outstretched, the long, flowing gowns billowing behind her as she walked out on stage. The audience was captivated, you could hear a pin drop. Her costume changes and the delivery of her repertoire was sensational. She was wonderful, the club was sold out and not a seat could be had. Many people were turned away. James and she became great friends and she remained loyal to him, never wanting to appear at the rival clubs which had sprung up. She was to return to Batley many times, always for a two-week run. She always sold out and she was ever the perfectionist.

She married an Italian man named Sergio Novak, who was also her manager. He was backstage one night standing in the tabs watching the show when he spilled his pint of beer into one of the speakers of the sound system. Miss Bassey's microphone went dead and she gestured her disgust by throwing her arms in the air and dropping the microphone, then walked off stage. She sat backstage waiting for the technicians to restore the sound. Eventually she returned in a new outfit saying to her audience, 'Well, a girl has to get changed,' thus covering up her new husband's accident. No doubt he was in for the ear whipping of his life, one that only she could deliver.

Chapter 7

Everybody Loves Somebody

Overleaf: Pauline and James.

Shortly after James bought his first Rolls Royce, Betty had to have one. She ordered a silver-blue convertible Corniche with a blue hood and looked the part of the millionaire she had become. James bought her a five carat diamond single stone ring. Her shopping trips into nearby Leeds were greeted with the utmost courtesy by the retailers she chose to patronise. She was treated like a VIP, spent money like water and enjoyed the bowing and scraping.

Not only did Betty want the best for herself and her home, her husband was to have a makeover by his wife. She noticed the latest styles worn by the top stars of the day and would not lose an opportunity of discovering who their tailors were and making appointments for James to be suited and booted by the best in the land. His image became as sharp as the artistes who appeared on stage. They were becoming the 'golden couple'.

Betty continued to be involved with the Victoria Bingo; she put a trustworthy manager in to run it, thus making sure her interests were well protected. It was always a busy place. She had learned that silver coinage before a certain date held more silver content than later coins and had her staff deliver all the two-shilling pieces and half crowns from the bingo to the house. She would sort through them on a daily basis; the early coins were saved in huge tins and lined up on a shelf in the cellar while the rest were returned to be banked. This ritual took place after she had got up for the day, usually at noon.

Whilst the business itself was on the crest of a wave, James and Betty were less than happy. The house was run by Sally and they had cleaners doing all the household chores. They doubled up as babysitters and little Jason was well taken care of, if lacking the affection he and Jamie were beginning to be starved of, due to the many distractions in their parents' successful life.

As Jason approached his first birthday, it was becoming obvious his growth was not as it should be. After a routine visit to a clinic, the resident nurse sympathetically brought the subject up on examining Jason. Betty already knew there was something not quite right. She was, however, burying her head in the sand, not wishing to face up to the problem. Eventually she sought a consultation with a paediatrician and he confirmed her worst fears, Jason's was a classic case of dwarfism. James and Betty were devastated.

They scoured the country trying to find help and a possible cure, eventually discovering a specialist in Switzerland. They made an appointment to fly out with Jason to see him. The specialist told them that the procedure to extend Jason's limbs would involve a very painful series of operations. His bones would be broken and extended. The whole procedure was experimental and no cure could be guaranteed. They flew back to the UK to consider the best course of action. After much deliberation and soul searching, neither was prepared to subject Jason to the months of torture he would have to endure. He was a very happy little fellow and they were determined he would stay that way. They loved him unconditionally, and though Jason's condition came as a great blow to his parents in the beginning, over time they accepted it was incurable.

As time went on he became quite a character, happy and extremely healthy. Betty had a stable block built for her two horses and bought a Shetland pony for Jason. At a nearby saddlers, she ordered a little seat to be specially made for her young son. It was a chair on which he could sit and be walked around the paddock. He loved it.

His grandmother Sally doted on her grandsons. She lived alone just down the road from her daughter in a little house bought by James and Betty. She walked to the cottage every morning to oversee the day-to-day running of the Corrigan household, saying that the exercise did her good. She was a blessing to Betty, always on hand to take over whenever she was needed. She would water the many plants dotted around the Corrigan house, usually over-watering them. Betty would take her to task trying to explain she was killing them with kindness. Sally would have none of it and carried on, knowing she knew better. When the poor plant was at the point of surrender, Betty would go buy another of the same kind, making sure it was a tad bigger, and put it in the place of the one it was replacing. When Sally noticed the new plant she would say to Betty, 'I told you these plants like my touch, just look how this plant has shot up'! Betty smiled to herself, allowing her mother to get one up on her.

Despite having a dream home, complete with a state of the art kitchen, Betty's idea of keeping it tidy was eating out. She rarely cooked. A Beefeater restaurant had opened shortly after the club; a very stylish place with an excellent menu and it was only a stone's throw away. It was easier to get in the car and drive down the road to eat. They went so often they had an account there. If they weren't feasting there, Betty would ring down to the club kitchen and have food sent to the house. There was always a constant flow of tea or coffee offered to anyone visiting the Corrigans. Visitors were made welcome and offered a hot drink poured into the best china; they never forgot their manners. But, other than that, the kitchen was out of bounds.

The larder in Oaks Cottage was a walk-in affair, there was enough food to feed an army; cases and cases of tinned food lined the walls. It was packed with everything imaginable, all bought at the local cash and carry in bulk. Betty would often buy for the bingo and while she was there would take the opportunity to fill the home at the same time. She would load the Rolls to capacity with her shopping exploits. The car was groaning on its axles by the time she had finished stacking it up.

Betty was beginning to resent James claiming all the credit for the club and ignoring the great contribution she had made. Also, she was seeing less and less of her husband as the weeks went by. The tension between the couple grew and their relationship became increasingly strained. James looked to Pauline for an escape route. Finding comfort in the arms of another woman was preferable to being in the middle of what were now almost constant rows at home. Betty was becoming more involved with the Cluskys. As James became cooler to her, she was becoming infatuated with Con. Betty was a very attractive woman. With the newfound wealth and financial independence came the freedom. The club may have been a brilliant success story but the reverse was happening to the Corrigan's marriage. Whilst they had the trappings of wealth, the once ideal partnership was going down the drain at an alarming rate.

James was an avid collector of all things military. His interest lay in the battles of yesterday and the arms which were used; guns, swords and battleaxes were lovingly displayed on the walls of his home. As the rows between the couple got worse, the use of a battleaxe or anything else to hand would come into play. Windows were smashed, furniture broken, the matrimonial front was worse than any battlefield. Often words failed them and it became physical, usually ending up with Betty locking herself in a bathroom and pretending to commit suicide. This was all play-acting but frighteningly convincing at the time. It was her way of stopping what was getting out of hand. Money was no problem to them so when the rows blew over, the damage would be repaired and all would be calm until the next uprising.

James watched the relationship between Betty and Con become ever closer. Being uncomfortable with it, he would challenge Betty and they would lock horns and row all night. She was beginning to get exhausted by these sessions and visited her doctor who prescribed sleeping capsules. She didn't use them for herself, but began lacing James's tea with the sleeping draft; emptying the contents of a couple of capsules into the liquid and putting extra sugar to disguise the taste. Her behaviour was very bizarre.

Betty's sister Mary had married a Jamaican and she'd gone to live there with her new husband. Jamaica was deeply into witchcraft and Mary told Betty that she could buy a spell to cast over James. Betty was hooked on all things paranormal, so suddenly black candles were burning in Oaks Cottage. The dining room, which was always suspected of being extra spooky, was being used to contact the dead. If any of the speciality acts playing Batley were into mind powers, they had an instant invitation to the house. Things got so bad that one morning when James was sat on the edge of the bed tying his shoe laces, he happened to see a doll with pins stuck in it under his side of the bed. He was mortified, thinking Betty was losing her marbles. This explained the many packages which had arrived from Jamaica. What else had she bought? Putting a spell on her husband sounds amusing, however James was not sure he could cope with voodoo!

Betty was feeling so insecure about her future that she saw her ventures into the world of the occult as her way of trying to find answers to questions which were beginning to trouble her. Was James having an affair? Was she going to find happiness with someone else? If so, who? She was looking to find the answer that she hoped for. She heard of a good fortune teller, so made an appointment and was advised to bring a possession owned by the person she was seeking to know the innermost thoughts of. She took a riding boot of Con's and a cuff link of James's. It was laughable really, but in another way sad. She was a very troubled soul. She gained no knowledge whatsoever by these trips to soothsayers, who consoled her with a few titbits of information, but never justified the fat fee paid. These were futile endeavours. However it kept her happy for a time.

Betty had become rich enough to buy anything she liked, with no demarcation line. She had so much money at her disposal it was a question of what could she do next and she was forever pouring over interior design books, looking for the latest craze. She came across a picture of a bedroom furnished with the most luxurious of silken drapes. The bed was adorned with expensive silk covers and pillows. The windows, cushions, everything was silk. She decided to turn their bedroom into what looked like a scene from *Arabian Nights*. James was horrified. He made his feelings known to his wife but it made no difference; the room was finished and that was the end of the matter as far as Betty was concerned. Their house was turning into a showpiece, not a home where James felt comfortable. He was to spend more and more time away.

Betty became suspicious of the trips away her husband was taking. When she found a hotel bill in his pocket from a trip she had no knowledge of, and other bits and pieces which made no sense to her, things were beginning to add up. One day the postman brought a letter. On opening it she discovered it related to an overlooked monthly payment on a Mini car. Puzzled, she confronted her husband but he denied all knowledge. It was the car he had bought for Pauline and he had forgotten to make the latest payment.

It was well known in the club that James was having a relationship, indeed Pauline had the run of the place. It seemed the only person not to know was Betty. James had wanted Pauline to be with him as often as possible. She had given up her job and was constantly on his arm whenever practical. Her sister was a hairdresser. James wanted Pauline to have a business of her own and acquired a rented shop close by her home and paid for it to be refurbished as a hairdressing salon. It was done out to perfection. Frankie Vaughan was appearing at the club at the time and when Pauline's new business was due to open, James asked Frankie to open the business, getting it off to a flying start.

Pauline was not a hairdresser. It was run by her sister. It gave her an income and, most of all, freedom to be with James. He was a controlling influence on all that she did. Slowly she was becoming trapped in a web of deceit.

Pauline and I were still firm friends and had lots of laughs at the high life she was living. When Pauline was not with James, we would eat out at a restaurant where James had an account, charging it all to him.

James went to the trouble of buying a caravan and put it in the car park at the back of the club. He used it as a rendezvous point where he could be with Pauline. It was a cosy little number where they could enjoy the privacy of being together. Betty never went around the back of the club. It was laughable.

Sometimes, when they were watching a show, James would get a member of staff to tell him he was wanted on the phone and, leaving Betty, he would pop through the back door, out to the car park and into the caravan where Pauline was waiting. Any stolen moments where they could be together were welcomed.

James was insanely jealous of his mistress and employed a detective to follow her home after the show finished. Not being trustful of this arrangement, he also engaged a detective to follow the detective! Pauline was suffocated by his insecurities. He would go to any lengths to spy on her, having the caravan bugged, listening in on her conversations, making sure she was staying faithful to him. Pauline and I would sometimes play cards in the caravan and we would see the bug under the table. Pauline would talk into it, mischievously saying how much she loved James and how faithful she was to him.

This kind of life was intolerable and Pauline was becoming a nervous wreck. She was being treated to anything her heart desired but what she really wanted was a more stable existence. It was all very well having everything a girl could want, but what she really wanted was not available to her. The man she had fallen in love with belonged to someone else.

One day James had been into Leeds to collect a diamond ring. On the way home he called in to see Pauline. He pulled the ring out of his pocket and asked her to try it on to see what it looked like. The diamond was huge, the size of a sixpence. Then came the punchline. 'It's a gift for Betty.' Pauline was speechless. How could he be so tactless? It was to lend the lie to the relationship. Pauline realised she was nothing more than a trophy on his arm when it suited him. He'd bought her a car and a house, all on extended terms, despite the fact he could have bought her the car and house outright. This was his way of keeping his mistress to himself. She was to be at his beck and call whenever he could find time to be with her. She could not see how to reverse out of the situation. If she had wanted to, she would become homeless, carless and financially destitute. A young woman in her twenties with her whole life in front of her was being suffocated. What was worse, the relationship was encouraged by her mother, no doubt blinded by the wealth. Alas, with wealth comes power and it was being exercised over her youngest daughter.

Betty was nobody's fool and it did not take long for her to spring into action. She did her own detective work by quizzing the staff at the club. She instilled the fear of God into them and, little by little, got to the bottom of what had been going on. With the revelation of her husband's extra-marital affair, it was game on; she became a woman possessed.

Her husband used private detectives but Betty needed none of these tactics. She was the most direct person you could wish to meet; she took the bull by the horns and looked you straight in the eyes. Getting at the truth was second nature to her. She discovered where Pauline's mother worked, tracked her down, and swore she would throw acid in her daughter's face when she found her. Pauline's mother was not a woman to be threatened and retaliated with vigour. The same day Betty went to the hairdressing salon, challenging her sister with more violent threats. More threats were thrown to other members of the family. Still, she could not find Pauline.

One evening Pauline and I were sat talking backstage when Betty must have heard a whisper that she was in the building. Bill, the stage manager, shouted to us, 'Get out of the way, she's got a gun.' We took to the toilets and both stood on the toilet seat with the door locked, thinking that if she looked under the door she would not see us. She burst through the stage door brandishing the gun, saying at the top of her voice, 'I know you are here. I will kill you when I get my hands on you.' We were absolutely terrified, hardly daring to breath. She was going from one room to another, thankfully not discovering our hiding place. Betty didn't find her, nor did she discover the caravan, but Pauline was so shocked by the experience that it took her days to recover.

Yet another row between Betty and James was to follow. They screamed abuse, accusing each other of the infidelities they had both committed. After what seemed like an age of out and out war, they both cooled down, confessing and confirming their relationships. Deciding to be adult, they agreed to continue with the relationships. Betty was to accept James's involvement with Pauline provided she could openly carry on her relationship with Con. They had called a truce. Pauline, after reassurances from James, was now free to be in the club openly.

Lulled into a false sense of security, shortly after these arrangements had been agreed, Pauline was sat watching a show when she felt the presence of someone at her side. On turning, she saw Betty was standing over her. She spat in her face and, without speaking a word, walked off. So much for the adult compromise. Her now possessive husband was about to be given the shock of his life. A woman scorned etc.

They were a couple at war and their children were the casualties having to endure the endless rows brought about by parents who were driven out of control by money and power. They were on the road to self-destruction. The marriage, which had been founded on love, was turning increasingly sour with each passing day. Just as Pauline was trapped, so too were James and Betty. Their business empire was huge and they both had too much to lose.

Pauline was in a state of near exhaustion. She had reached the end as far as the relationship with James was concerned and she told him she was calling an end to the affair. Whatever had been arranged between Betty and himself was not working out and she wanted her freedom. They remained friends, parting on the best of terms. For the sake of her sanity she had to free herself from not just James, but the threats from his wife which put her in fear of her life.

Betty liked to throw parties afterhours and would ask the kitchen staff to prepare sandwiches and nibbles. When the show was over and all the people had left, the piano was wheeled out onto the middle of the stage, the lid closed and the top used for the prepared food. Drinks were flowing and the hospitality could not have been better. They were wonderful parties. Usually the artistes who were appearing were there, there'd be lots of music and dance. A good time was had by all. James, however, being teetotal, was more concerned about the safety of the piano. After a few drinks, the guests were less than careful. He never let his hair down, much to the annoyance of Betty.

It was times like these which would spark the arguments, usually with James storming out and going home only to lie in wait for Betty when she finally arrived back. Not only did he not approve of the piano being used as a table, he did not approve of his wife enjoying herself with the artistes. He was a very jealous man. Despite his own infidelity, the same rules did not apply to Betty.

Lennie Bennett was a guest at one of these parties. He and Betty disappeared for a short time. This was noted by James. He challenged them on their return. He was certain something was going on between them and he cornered Lennie in his office, who denied being anything other than honourable, claiming he had only taken Betty for a coffee. This explanation did not pacify James. He became violent and threatened him with a knife. Fortunately the threats subsided, but Lennie was in a state of shock, thinking James was about to stab him. He never worked the club again.

James had a great deal on his mind. It was becoming clear there were not enough top rate artistes to fill the club on a nightly basis. His timing had been extremely lucky; he had a knack of engaging artistes who, when they were due to appear at Batley, had a record in the charts or a television show appearance, which of course heightened the interest of the public. Everyone by now had heard of Batley, he had put the town well and truly on the map. The top names in show business had worked the club or were about to work it; it was easier to say who had not appeared there than who had. James was proud to be the champion of the working man, his was not a club for the stuffy, cultured classes but for the masses, they were not given the mediocre but the very best from the world of show business. But running the club and keeping that momentum up was becoming a monumental task.

Chapter 8

Bring Me Sunshine

Overleaf: James with waiting staff.

My first dubious encounter with the national press came when we arranged the appearance of an artiste called Tiny Tim. He was a very strange man from America who brought with him a lady friend by the name of 'Miss Vicki'. His claim to fame was a cover of a very old song called 'Tiptoe Through the Tulips' which had entered the UK charts. His act comprised of him standing on stage with a megaphone singing the old songs from the war era. He'd sing 'It's a Long Way to Tipperary' and '(There'll Be Bluebirds Over) The White Cliffs of Dover' while Miss Vicki stood at the corner of the stage looking on. She had no part to play other than standing there looking like Olive Oyl out of a Popeye cartoon. They had to be the most peculiar couple ever.

Tiny Tim had just walked out on stage on the opening night when I was called to the telephone. A reporter asked if I would like to comment on a recent incident where a member of the audience had given Tiny Tim a punch in the face, allegedly being offended that this American freak was taking the piss out of our war heroes by singing all the songs the British public hold dear. I looked at the telephone puzzled. I told the reported there had not been an incident and he was talking nonsense. He was most apologetic, saying he must have got his wires crossed.

I returned to the club to see the rest of the act and saw a man get up from the audience to assault Tiny Tim. It was clearly a put-up job for the purpose of publicity, a pre-arranged stunt to make the front pages of the following day's newspapers. Whoever had tipped the press off had been premature; the informant had jumped the gun. It was a spectacular stunt which went spectacularly wrong. The plant was shown the door which meant that Tiny Tim had got a fist in the face for nothing. We all knew it was a set up, the audiences at Batley would never have assaulted anyone. They may have thrown pennies or shown their displeasure at an artiste who was going down badly, but would never resort to violence. The club was known as being family friendly and there had never been any sign of trouble during the heady days of its hey day.

There were countless stories for the press coming from the now famous club, all due to the Corrigan tenacity. James decided to tempt Gracie Fields out of retirement. He went to Capri, an island off the coast of Italy where she had chosen to spend her retirement with her husband Boris. Rumour had it she owned the entire island. She had not appeared in public for years. By now she was an old lady.

James tried to tempt her back on to the stage by offering her two weeks at Batley. She was forever in the nation's heart as 'Our Gracie' and James thought it would be a nice sentimental journey for her, not to mention another coup for him and his club. Mr Corrigan could be most persuasive and charming, it was difficult to refuse him anything and so eventually she agreed to appear.

Dusting off her music, she arrived for her band call on the due date. She looked like a frail old lady. James began to have second thoughts when he saw her. On the same show was a very strong club act by the name of Ronnie Dukes and Riki Lee. James plucked the courage up to go into Gracie's dressing room and ask if she would close the first half of the show so that her fans from Rochdale, her home town in Lancashire, could leave after her appearance as they had a long journey back. This was the most diplomatic excuse he could think of for not putting her on at the top of the bill, where she should have been. 'Just as you like love,' she said.

When Gracie Fields walked out onto the stage on opening night, she had shed years. She looked wonderful; her make-up perfect, her hair beautifully coiffured. When she started to sing, it became abundantly clear she had lost none of her magic. The audience went wild. She sang her old favourites one after

Joey with John Edwin in 1940.

James in the Merchant Navy.

James calling the bingo numbers.

James with Jason.

Jamie presents a key to The Bachelors on opening night.

The iconic sign at the club.

Jason presenting flowers to the Duchess of Kent. Proud mum Betty looks on.

Me with Joe Brown and a nurse at a Clayton Hospital concert.

Celebrating my birthday at the club with champagne.

Me and Gene Pitney.

A signed photo from the great Satchmo.

Lulu, her mum and sister with Betty and James.

Shirley Bassey, undisputed Queen of Batley, on stage at the club.

James and Betty at the wedding of Jamie and Janet.

Elaine and James with Marilyse, Sheralyn and Annalisa.

another, the audience were on their feet cheering, shouting, clapping, you name it. They adored her, she was sensational. Eventually, and reluctantly, she was allowed to leave the stage. To follow this was Dukes and Lee. They were wasting their time. Their act paled into insignificance. They could not follow the great Gracie Fields, who had not lost her sparkle.

In the audience that first night was Jess Yates, producer of *Stars on Sunday*, a light religious programme made by Yorkshire Television. He went backstage and signed her up for the 'God Spot' as it was known in the business. She was perfect for his Sunday audiences and went on to make many appearances. The ever popular Gracie was once again a firm favourite, another artiste who benefited from the Corrigan magic.

After the first night's performance, James had the unenviable task of going to see Ms Fields and finding the right words to reverse the running order. He told her that Dukes and Lee would close the first half of the show as they needed to go off to perform elsewhere. That was a little white lie. James was tripping over his words and sounding more and more implausible. After he bumbled out his reasons for the change, Gracie said, 'Just as you like love.' As he came away he sensed she knew quite well why she was closing the show.

She was a sensation. The two weeks went so well, the roads from Rochdale were a coach cavalcade, all heading across the Pennines to see their own home-grown superstar. She was their darling and could do no wrong. On the last night, James went into Gracie's dressing room to congratulate her on her success and invited her to make a return visit. 'Yes love,' she replied, 'but it will be double the fee.' She never did return.

James had his share of temperamental artistes and coping with them sometimes required the patience of a saint. One of the most difficult was P.J. Proby. He was a buck Texan who had made it big with a couple of hit records. His image was that of Beau Brummell; he wore very tight, black velvet pants and his hair was tied back in a ponytail with a velvet bow. His real name was

Jim Smith. His fame had been built on his stage act which was so energetic that it usually resulted in him tearing his trousers. This, believe it or not, made national news. Everyone wanted to see him perform.

He turned up at the club on a Sunday afternoon with a bottle of wine in his hand, totally drunk. His manager was making excuses for the state of his artiste and reassured everyone that he would be sober later that evening. He was in no fit state to have a band call; he could hardly stand up, let alone sing.

When it came to his first performance, he was less inebriated but still under the influence. His act was so bad the audience booed him. Proby started hurling insults back. The club was in uproar. In desperation, Proby told the audience, 'If you don't like it, go and demand your money back!' Allan Clegg, the poor club manager, on hearing this locked himself in the office and put the 'engaged' sign on the door. There was no way any refunds would be given.

James called P.J. and his manager into his office and Mr Proby got the biggest dressing down of his life. Apologising profusely, Proby's manager said how sorry and embarrassed he was. 'I could dig a hole and bury myself.' James told him to dig it a bit deeper and, pointing at Proby, 'Put him in it!'

James was planning on paying Proby off, he wanted no more of this drunken singer. The following day the agents in London were alerted to what had happened. Proby's manager pleaded with James to give him another chance, saying the agents would send the secretary from the office to come and sort him out. James reluctantly agreed.

The secretary arrived and by this time Proby had sobered up. She guarded him with her life and kept him away from the bottle. She washed his hair and got him cleaned up. When he walked out on stage looking like the P.J. Proby the audience expected to see, he said, 'The bastards wont let me have a drink.' The stage manager chalked a mark on the floor of the stage and told him not to move off it if he valued his life!

All went well with the show, he did as he was told and gave

a solid performance. He was a great singer, just sadly out of control. He clearly had a drink problem and had to be guarded to protect him from himself. But, despite the best efforts of his minders to keep him away from the bottle, he would find a way to outfox them. He carried on and honoured his contract but when he finally left, the staff heaved a sigh of relief. He was so unpredictable.

Gordon Mills, the manager of Tom Jones and Englebert Humperdink, agreed to the appearance of Englebert. He was another amazing act, only this time for all the right reasons. As the week went by, Tom Jones came along with his entourage to see the show and, I suppose, to see what the club was like. He sat on the balcony surrounded by his bodyguards, which was all very unnecessary really. Halfway through his act, Humperdink stopped and announced to the audience that Tom Jones was on the balcony. This was a big mistake. After they knew he was there, they stopped watching Humperdink and craned their necks to get a glimpse of Tom.

Tom Jones was also to appear at Batley around Christmas time. He turned up with his friend Marjorie Wallace, a former Miss World who was stripped of her title once it went public that she was liaising with the married singer. On the last night of the run, some of the staff were dressed up. They had been invited to a private fancy dress party after the show and Tom Jones asked if he could go. It was strictly fancy dress and, as he had none, he was refused. He also sent a message to James asking him if he would like to go backstage to his dressing room to meet Miss Wallace. James was really busy and declined the invitation.

The next morning, James was in his office when in came one of the cleaning ladies to tell him that the star's dressing room was in a hell of a mess. James went down to see what she was talking about; the place had been trashed, there was white powder all over the walls, everything was broken. It turned out the white powder was from a fire extinguisher which had been let off. In the waste bin was a piece of cardboard, the kind used on the inside of a shirt wrapper. Written on it was a message. 'You have a liking for practical jokes James, how about this one, now clean this fucking mess up.' It was torn in half and discarded in the bin.

Obviously Tom had had second thoughts about leaving the message. We assumed this awful behaviour was due to him feeling snubbed by staff and James for not wishing to join him for drinks. Fortunately the club was closed the following week so there was time for the damage to be repaired, but James was furious. He went back to his office and called the Queens Hotel in Leeds and asked if Tom had left. He was told that Tom was still in bed and was due to leave around 4pm.

James drove over to the Queens Hotel knowing Tom's car was the limousine version of a Rolls Royce. He found it in the car park and proceeded to let all the tyres down. He knew that with this kind of vehicle, it would be difficult to get it back on the road. James wrote a message and left it under a windscreen wiper. It read, 'Guess who!'

James rang the following day to find out what time they had eventually left the hotel. It was 8.30pm so James was pleased that he had inconvenienced him by four and a half hours. That was the last time Tom Jones ever worked Batley. In fact, his name was taboo.

To appear at Batley was to be afforded hospitality, courtesy and facilities second to none. There was always a well-stocked complementary bar in the star's dressing room and a backstage manager to make sure all was as it should be. The artistes were looked after and given every consideration for the duration of their stay. To abuse that hospitality was a great shame.

Bruce Forsyth was booked to appear on the same show as David Whitfield. David was the first to arrive on the Sunday afternoon for a band call and he was pleased to see his name in lights outside the club. He had been given joint billing with Bruce Forsyth. When Bruce arrived later, he saw the billing and made it clear to the management that he was top of the bill and his name must appear larger. David Whitfield's name was changed to smaller letters.

James, feeling embarrassed, explained to David what had happened and apologised. James had no time for anyone with an overinflated ego, no matter who they were. As far as he was concerned they were there to do a job. David was most understanding. However, when he went on stage, he sang his heart out, giving it his all and making sure Mr Forsyth would have his work cut out trying to follow him. Indeed it was not a happy week for Bruce Forsyth, he was eclipsed by the Talented Mr Whitfield.

The public were becoming spoilt for choice and were being very selective as to who they would see. The weekends were usually booked up, but midweek presented problems. This is where I came in with the complementary tickets, which had to be done discreetly. I was kept busy working closely with the booking office, monitoring the forward bookings. I approached the many factory sports and social secretaries in the area, suggesting they apply for tickets for their workers. From the club's point of view, this made perfect sense as once they were inside the club, they would be drinking and eating. The theory was that half a loaf was better than none and it made for a better atmosphere all around. To aim for a capacity audience, coach companies were given concessionary tickets for the midweek shows. It was mutually beneficial.

The use of the complementary tickets was to be kept a secret, which was all very well but at times it worked against us. A conversation was overheard between a well known comedy double act, Mike & Bernie Winters. One was saying to the other, 'We have had a wonderful week, working to capacity crowds. When we are asked to do a return booking, we must ask for more money.' The truth was, the bookings were so poor that a record number of complementary tickets had been given out.

When this conversation was revealed to James and it was suggested that it might be a good idea to let these artistes know the true state of their pulling power, James would not hear of it. Ever the gentleman, he was not about to burst their balloon, nor anyone else's for that matter. This was not in his nature. If they left feeling good about themselves then he was pleased. He would deal with the financial demands in his own way. He was proud to be the owner of such a successful venue and he was not about to give away any trade secrets. In truth, I was to put more bums on seats than most of the artistes.

There are many glitches to overcome when running a club, and to do so without the public's knowledge was a mark of the professionalism of the management. Illness, however, was a fact which could not be ignored. Morecambe and Wise were playing to sell out audiences. Ernie Wise was staying at the Queens Hotel in Leeds. Eric, who never stayed at the same hotel as Ernie, had booked into the Selby Fork Motel, which was quite a long drive from the club. One night, Eric was enjoying a drink after the show. He had joined a number of the staff and myself who were playing a game of cards. We all enjoyed his company and had a great laugh with him, he was as funny off stage as he was on and had the ability to cheer up the most miserable of souls. The conversation turned to the topic of his digs for the week, and he told us that he had not realised the amount of driving that would be involved when he booked the Selby Fork. He was taking the long way around the countryside to avoid traffic. Allan Clegg suggested that he drive through the centre of Leeds because after midnight when he came off stage there would be very little traffic.

When it was time for Eric to leave, he invited me to a party at his hotel. Naively, I asked how many would be going. 'Just you and I,' he replied. I declined. He then asked me if he could run me home. I declined that invitation too. Allan said I was a spoil sport and should let him run me home. We'd had a few drinks and the banter was wild. Eventually I was talked into the offer of a lift.

We left in his Jensen car. He duly delivered me home, only a mile from the club. We sat talking for a while at the gate. When he was about to leave, he turned and gave me a goodnight kiss.

He took the new route suggested by Allan, but he began to feel ill as he approached the centre of Leeds. He pulled the car over and hailed a pedestrian, explained he was having chest pains and asked if he could help. That man was Eric's saviour, he put him in the passenger seat and drove him to Leeds General Infirmary. He was having a massive heart attack. Fortunately they were on the doorsteps of the leading cardiology unit in the country. They saved his life. One dreads to think what would have been the outcome if he had gone through the country lanes that night. He would not have seen a soul and the outcome might have been very different.

Back at the club, the staff were heartbroken at the news. When we learned what had happened, it was action stations to try and find a replacement artiste to close the show. No one could step into the shoes of Morecambe and Wise. The management was devastated at the thought of Eric being at death's door, none more so than me. I could not help thinking what would have happened if I had accepted the invitation to go with him to the Selby Fork Motel. I would have been the one to be with him in the car, what would that have looked like!

All the London agencies were called, but to find someone at such short notice was almost impossible. Eventually, Miss Joan Turner agreed to finish the week. It was very brave of her to take the job. She was a serious singer with a wonderful voice, more suited to the opera stage than Batley. But she was available and courageously volunteered her services.

Refunds were demanded by the public and given, with no questions asked. It was organised chaos. I and one of the office staff worked through the night, making the arrangements for the new show. There were just two of us in the office, getting complementary tickets printed ready to be given out to anyone who could make use of them. The club took on a life of its own that night. The strangest of noises were being heard. The place was almost coming to life. It was explained later that the heat was contracting all the crisp wrappers that littered the club. It was an eerie feeling and we were scared. We were not happy bunnies, being tired and in need of sleep. I didn't sleep for two days and nights. However, Eric was recovering, and if a standing ovation could be given for that fact alone, he would have got one. The staff were overjoyed he was making a full recovery.

Many lasting and fleeting relationships were born in the club; couples met their future partners and romances were commonplace. When the Bee Gees played, Maurice Gibb, one of the brothers who had recently been divorced from Lulu, met and fell in love with one of the waitresses. She was a very beautiful girl named Yvonne Spenceley. She took drinks backstage and when Maurice saw her, he went starry eyed. It was love at first sight. Within a month they were married and Yvonne was living a completely different lifestyle to that of a waitress. She was whisked off to Miami in Florida, living the life of a superstar's wife. They were happily married and stayed together until Maurice died prematurely of a heart attack many years later.

The Bee Gees were another act who had not worked a club before. Their management requested that the show be announced as 'The Bee Gees in Concert'. Maurice always spoke highly of the club, they had been treated like kings and he had found the love of his life there.

Another star who found a match was Roy Orbison, who met his wife in a discothèque in Leeds. He was a very sad man, having lost his wife to cancer. Shortly after this tragedy he lost two sons in a house fire at his home in America. He was on tour at the time. After doing his act at Batley, he went into Leeds to Cinderella Rockafellas and met Barbara. Again it was love at first sight. They tied the knot and lived happily until they were parted by Roy's death.

Roy was a regular visitor to the club, he enjoyed working there. He also stayed at the Corrigans. He had the run of the place and he could stay in bed as long as he wanted, usually all day. He was not to be disturbed by anything.

Many artistes preferred staying at Oaks Cottage rather than staying in hotels or the showbiz digs. One such guest was Eartha

Kitt. She was a lovely lady, famous for her sexy feline charms when singing. Her purring persona on stage was the opposite of her true personality. She was a very clever lady, warm hearted, and her priorities were firmly entrenched in being humane. Materialism was an act. Her priorities lay in the true things in life, not the material. She had her young daughter travelling with her. Her name was Kitt. Whilst doing her show dates, Eartha was guiding her with values that were real. Show business was an illusion, not to be taken seriously.

One morning, Betty was at the table in the dining room going through the silver from the previous night's takings at the bingo hall. Jason was walking about with a wet nappy down to his ankles and feeding from a bottle of milk in his mouth. Eartha, seeing this, was incensed. She went to the table with outstretched hand and swept the money off it, sending it flying across the room. She told Betty that her son needed her attention, that she was a mother first and a businesswoman second. Betty was astounded, she was not used to being spoken to like that, but she duly took care of Jason, making sure she did not repeat the mistake, at least for the duration of Eartha Kitt's stay.

Eartha made a trip to Batley market, which took place on a Friday afternoon. The many stalls were lined up, selling everything one could wish for, and the stall holders shouted out, challenging the town's folk to buy their wares. Eartha was intrigued. She soon had a crowd around her, all wanting to have a chat, or a signed autograph of the American singer. She was a very sexy lady but had a very down to earth approach to life and loved the banter with the locals. She asked them what they liked to sing. The shoppers taught her the words of 'On Ilkla Moor Baht 'at'. They told her it was the national anthem of Yorkshire. The Batley folk could not wait to sing for the great Eartha. She became the conductor of the community sing-song and brought the market to a standstill.

Just as the stage in the club had the most famous feet in show business treading the boards, the cobbles of Batley market were getting their share too. Danny La Rue brought his complete show to Batley. With him came a troupe of dancers, or his 'boys and girls' as he called them. His costumes were out of this world; the remarkable make-up and wigs transformed him from a male into a female, defying anyone to know he was a man. Where he disguised his manhood was a mystery. He had a pair of legs any woman would have died for; he was better looking in drag than any woman.

Danny had never worked a club before, except his own, which was a tiny, intimate club in Hanover Square in London. It had a small stage in one corner and he appeared after midnight, performing his wonderful drag act. His audiences stayed until breakfast, when the waiters placed a tablecloth on the tables, removed any drinks and served bacon and eggs.

The show was amazing. He was booked for a three-week run, staying with James and Betty. Whilst staying with the Corrigans, James and he became great friends. He loved being in the town. He would walk to the club from Oaks Cottage with a freshly laundered shirt over his arm, chatting to the locals on his way. It was only about a mile, downhill all the way. The locals loved the interaction. There was nothing pretentious about Danny.

One of the national papers worked out how many basket meals and pints of beer had to be sold to pay for his show; it was a mountain of chips, an ocean of scampi and a river of beer. It must have taken the *Daily Mail* forever to work all that out but it amused Danny when he read it. When he'd finished his run, he was very sorry to leave. He had enjoyed his appearance at the venue and also the generous hospitality of his hosts. On the last night of his appearance, James gave him the gift of a gold watch. A very thin time piece, it must have cost a fortune. Danny was overwhelmed by the gesture.

Chapter 9

Give Me The Moonlight

Overleaf: James at his desk.

Batley was playing cupid to the visiting stars and public alike, with many couples meeting and falling in love. It was romance all the way, a star-studded playground with many of the artistes standing at the bar to chat the pretty girls up after their spot. However, if the world was falling in love at Batley, it was having the opposite effect on the Corrigans.

James had booked the American songwriter Neil Sedaka. Neil had been a big name in the fifties but his star was on the wane in the late sixties. He came to England in the hope of doing a few cabaret dates. He was not commanding a large sum of money. The week's engagement proved hugely successful. The audiences loved him. James took him under his wing, trying to promote him by telling the agents in London how good the business had been. Batley had become a highly respected venue. If the artistes did well, it was a step up the ladder.

James offered Neil his hospitality at Oaks Cottage. Whilst staying with James and Betty, he overheard them having a heated argument. When these two got going it was hard to know when it would stop. As tempers cooled, they all sat down with a cup of tea around the kitchen table. Neil, trying to be the peacemaker, asked what was happening to them. The unhappy couple related how, before the club came along, they had been such a close and happy family. They told him they had been much better without all the glitz and glamour which, as far as they were concerned, had removed them from the reality of life. Betty went so far as to say the business was tearing them apart. They talked long into the night with Neil trying to play advocate; he was a very sensitive man, feeling so very sorry to see what was troubling them. Being in the marital home he could sense the deep hurt between the two.

A day after this night of soul searching, Neil sat around the table with them and pulled out a manuscript. He had penned a song for them and handed the score to Betty. 'The Hungry Years' was the story of their lives. He had written on the score, 'To Betty, no copyright reserved. Love, Neil.' He had captured their story. Later he was to include the song in an album called *Overnight Success*. When the album was released in the United States, it was renamed *The Hungry Years*.

'The Hungry Years'

Girl we made it to the top
We went so high we couldn't stop
We climbed the ladder leading us nowhere
Two of us together
Building castles in the air.

We spun so fast we couldn't tell
The gold ring from the carousel
How could we know the ride would turn out bad
Everything we wanted
Was everything we had.

I miss the hungry years
The once upon a time
The lovely long ago
We didn't have a dime
Those days of me and you
We lost along the way.

How could I be so blind not to see the door
Closing on the world
I now hunger for
Looking through my tears
I miss the hungry years.

We shared our daydreams one by one
Making plans was so much fun
We set our goals and reached the highest star

The things that we were after
Were much better from afar.

Here we stand just me and you
With everything and nothing too
It wasn't worth the price we had to pay
Honey take me home
Let's go back to yesterday.

I miss the hungry years
The once upon a time
The lovely long ago
We didn't have a dime
Those days of me and you
We lost along the way.

How could I be so blind
Not to see the door
Closing on the world
I now hunger for
Looking through my tears
I miss the hungry years
I miss the hungry years

After giving the words to Betty, Neil started singing the song. She was almost moved to tears and James was speechless. The friendship firmly sealed, one of the most prolific songwriters in the world had paid them a great compliment by dedicating a song to them. Later it was to become one of his greatest hits.

During this time, Neil and Betty went shopping together in Leeds. Neil was sporting a scruffy tracksuit, not bothering to make an effort to get changed. They went in Betty's Rolls Royce, with heads turning on the way to Leeds. She had the hood down, giving the public an opportunity to see the top of the bill at Batley. They had a great time shopping together, Betty taking him to her favourite shops. When they got home, they sat having a chat over a cup of tea. Neil told Betty how much he had enjoyed the trip and meeting the people of Leeds. Betty replied, 'Well, actually Neil, I was a little embarrassed at the state of your dress, you do look a little scruffy, more like a ragamuffin than the top of the bill at my club.' Neil was speechless, realising he should have tried to look the part of the superstar. It was a compliment to Betty that he could feel so relaxed in her company. He could be himself after spending most of his time in stage costumes.

Neil Sedaka was to return to America, James urging him to play Las Vegas. He could help him as he now had many contacts in the States. Neil went back to his homeland and played the cabaret rooms there. His star was in the ascendancy again. Neil was reborn, his talents renewed, reversing his failing career. He was back on top thanks to the Corrigans.

The club was a busy place with people coming and going and there was always some gossip going on between the staff. They were happy days. James's brother John Edwin was a frequent visitor. John lived in Bridlington and worked a prize bingo stall for one of his friends. He carried on the showman tradition, often having fun with the holidaymakers between games of bingo, chatting and telling with pride how he was the brother of the famous James Corrigan. John Edwin never had a family of his own and he loved Jamie and Jason as his own children. They loved Uncle Johnny in return and he spent lots of time with them.

Unknown to James, John Edwin installed French letter machines in the gents' toilets. No one questioned it, thinking he had done this with James's permission. He would fill the machines with 'something for the weekend sir'! This went on for weeks, with John Edwin making regular visits to collect the money and restock the machines. When emptying the money, he used large cloth cash bags and made sure he serviced his little sideline when James was out of the club. He was doing good business. One day when he was emptying the machines he took Jason along to help. Jason was now four years old and was pulling the money bag behind him. It was so heavy with the silver coins he could barely drag it along the carpeted floor. Unexpectedly, James walked in the club and asked what his son was doing with all the money? John Edwin had to confess and the game was up on his little sideline. James hit the roof and made him remove the machines. Poor little Jason burst into tears when his father was shouting at his favourite uncle, being far too young to know or understand what was happening. What made matters worse, John Edwin had been buying 'seconds' to maximise his profits. James was in fear of being sued thinking there may be a number of unwanted pregnancies around the town. He did eventually see the funny side after he had calmed down.

Frankie Vaughan was a frequent visitor to the club, though his first appearance left James with egg on his face. His management in London had asked for a car to be hired for the duration of his stay. He was staying with his sister and brother-in-law in an area of Leeds known as Alwoodley. This was predominantly a Jewish community, indeed Frankie's family were decedents of Russian Jews. A Mercedes was booked, delivered to his sister's house and parked in the drive. There was shock and horror when they saw the make of car and a phone call was made to the club. 'This car must be returned immediately, to be replaced by an English vehicle.' It was pointed out that due to the war and the way the Germans had mistreated the Jews, no self-respecting Jew would be seen with anything German, particularly a car. The mistake was soon rectified and all was well. Frankie was forgiving and years later was to laugh about the incident, saying his sister nearly got drummed out of Leeds when the neighbours saw it pulling up at their house.

When Frankie went on stage he was played on with the song 'Give Me the Moonlight'. He had a cane under his arm and would wear a top hat, doing a high kick and doffing his hat at the audience. Bernie Clifton, a comedian on the same bill, as a joke pretended to make an entrance with a cane under his arm; the joke was the cane was an extra-long one and when he walked out the end of the cane would follow. At the end of the cane was a flue brush, used by chimney sweeps, that was to be the gag. The backstage boys had found some drain rods and for a laugh extended the cane without Bernie's knowledge. He walked out onto the stage with the cane under his arm and carried on walking. The cane kept coming so he had to walk down the steps, off the stage and into the audience. He carried on walking, waiting for the end of the cane to appear. He was out of the club and onto Bradford Road before it eventually arrived. Everyone was in stitches, including Frankie Vaughan. The joke was on Bernie.

James had for some time been trying to engage Cliff Richard, who had never worked a club. He was very hesitant to work there for reasons of his faith; it meant working Sunday and Cliff never worked Sundays. He had his Christian principles and Batley was open seven nights a week. After much persuasion from James, he eventually agreed to work the week, but in doing so he asked the management to donate what would have been his fee for the Sunday night to charity. James put his Rolls Royce at Cliff's disposal for the duration of his stay, for which he was most grateful. He was well looked after by the management and the show was sold out. His audiences went wild the minute he walked on stage. He was a true gentleman and a joy to be around.

Tommy Cooper was a very funny man. When he was due to appear, the management sent a car to collect him from Leeds Bradford airport. It was a journey of about fifteen miles and should have taken no more than an hour, but hours later they still had not arrived. Eventually they turned up and it was discovered that the delay was caused by Tommy insisting they stop at every pub along the way, saying to the driver, 'If you mix your drinks, you never get drunk.'

He insisted on a band call but it was never understood why; he was simply to be played on stage to 'The Sheik of Araby'. He met the band and, before they could start, he insisted they all have a drink, then another, and another … By the time his rehearsal was over, they were all drunk. On the last night of his show he asked for two empty crates to be delivered from the bar to his dressing room. Thinking he wanted them as props for his act, they were sent. He needed them to put all the bottles from his complementary bar. He cleared it out, even the tonic waters, then put the crates in the back of his car, ready for departure.

The landscape around the towns surrounding Batley was changing. The mills were slowly closing and the workers paid off as orders for woollen cloth were going elsewhere. The Far East could turn out the materials much cheaper. Also, manmade fabrics had taken over from the traditional natural cloths made for centuries in the heavy woollen district and the home market was shrinking. It was a slow decay creeping across the industrial north, leaving mills idle. One such mill stood derelict with broken windows. An American singer, Billy Daniels, had been booked to do a week at the club. James collected him from the airport and drove him to the venue. He was chatting to James on the journey saying this was his first time in the north of England and he did not know what to expect. This gave James an idea to play a trick. Instead of driving him to the club, he drove him to one of the derelict mills. Pulling up outside the wreck of a building, he turned to Billy and announced, 'Well, what do you think of it?' In disbelief, Billy said, 'Is this it?' The look on his face was pure panic. 'Just joking,' said James, then he turned the Rolls Royce around and took him to the real venue. The joke was enjoyed by both, great relief flooding across the face of the unsuspecting artiste.

Amid the urban sprawl, and in the most unlikely of places, people took a drive to see the famous building, which looked very unexciting from the outside. It was when one walked through the doors, with the lights going down and the music striking up, when it became a magical place. It was a cross between a club and a theatre. The club had successfully put the audience in touch with the entertainers by crossing the divide of the orchestra pit, which the theatres used to separate the audience from the performers. No longer did the artistes have to look out and see nothing but a black void, they could reach out and touch somebody's hand, and often did. The physical contact with the audience was a first.

Ken Dodd always loved appearing, saying Yorkshire audiences love to laugh. 'Have you ever been tickled missus? Have you ever been tickled at Batley?' Ken loved the place so much he would stand there telling jokes and making his audiences laugh for hours at a time. He refused to leave the stage. Whilst the audience sat there enjoying themselves, he was not going to walk away.

James knew what people wanted. Isn't that a great thing, to know what people want and then say, 'I will build it and you'll like it'? And they did. The management at Batley were also a happy camp. For such a large operation, keeping the wheels on the track was achieved by a small band of hard-working people, all of whom had acquired experience by trial and error, with very little of the latter. They were always happy to help in any way they could and this feeling of wellbeing spread to the artistes. They knew they were supported by the very best in the way of musicians, sound effects, lighting and anything which showed them to their very best advantage. This was all par for the course at Batley.

There was great deal of talented artistes on the doorstep. One such artiste was Sammy King. He entertained with his band around the clubs; he was a very talented songwriter, often performing at Batley. He was a friend of all at the club and was held in high esteem. Sammy had a long career in music and had been managed at one time by Bernard Hinchcliffe and had a record out, but there'd been a big break in his career when he suffered a nervous breakdown. It was a slow recovery for him, but it was helped greatly by a chance encounter with James.

One day, Sammy bumped into James outside the club; at this stage Sammy still couldn't work and had no money. James asked him how he was feeling and Sammy told him that he was starting to feel better. James took him for a walk round the perimeter of the club and asked him what he wanted to do next. Sammy explained that he was thinking of getting an act together and playing again. Without hesitation, James told him that if he did get an act together then he would give him a spot at the club. 'You don't need to audition. If it's you and whoever else, then

'I'm sure it will be good enough.' This was an important vote of confidence for Sammy and when he got his act together, true to his word, James gave him two weeks at the club and Sammy was back on his feet again.

He started to write some new songs and later, when Roy Orbison came to the club, Sammy got a chance to play a cassette of his songs to Roy. Amongst these songs was the aptly named 'Penny Arcade'. When Roy Orbison got back to America he recorded it and it became a huge hit.

Sammy though, kept his feet firmly on the ground. A representative from the American agency which recorded Roy Orbison flew over to try and tempt Sammy to go to America, offering a lucrative contract to work in the States. Sammy was having none of it. He was the least materialistic man you could wish to meet and was very happy in his native Yorkshire. The glitter of America held no appeal. He had everything he needed in Batley, where he had lived all his life. He owned a small recording studio, which local artistes made good use of. All in all, he was happy with his lot and saw no reason to change his life by going to a strange land.

The resident musicians were another great bunch of talent, and were often tempted away to join the many artistes appearing at Batley as their musical directors. Freddie Starr, a regular at the club who brought with him his own particular brand of humour, was totally unpredictable and had the place in uproar. Freddie managed to tempt away Ted Platt, the lead guitarist of the resident orchestra. Ted was a very talented musician and musical arranger. He went on the road with Freddie as his musical director and they stayed together for many years. Danny La Rue engaged another local talent, Frannie (Francis) Haywood, who was a highly-regarded drummer. Again he was to have a long and happy working relationship with Danny.

Often the artistes such as Shirley Bassey would want a big line-up of musicians to augment the house band. With Leeds College of Music almost on the doorstep, there was a pool of talented musicians who could read the many parts the artistes' musical directors brought with them. They could lift the roof and looked forward to the call whenever they were needed.

One artist, an Australian by the name of Martin St James, arrived as a support act. He had a half-hour slot as a mind reader and went down really well with the audience. In reality, he was a hypnotist. When the management heard this they gave him top billing, booking him for his hypnotist routine. Putting him top of the bill was a big gamble to take, no one had heard of him. But the management had made the right move, he was sensational. And, not being a big name, he was low budget which was an added bonus.

His act involved getting a number of people from the audience onto the stage and hypnotising them. He made suggestions with the prompt of certain music, each person having their own musical cue. They would become outrageous characters such as men performing ballet, or chickens strutting, or kissing the person next to them. The show was a hit and was packing the place. News of this very funny act was travelling fast. He was slick and every night it was a different show as the volunteers reacted differently. It was truly hilarious. Batley was to make Martin St James a very big name in club land. He would appear for three weeks at a time and fill the place. He went from strength to strength. Then disaster struck.

Martin was appearing in a show in the North East of England. A man who had attended his show and been hypnotised had returned home and committed suicide. It was curtains for Martin, the papers had a picture of his eyes with the headline 'Did These Eyes Kill?' The papers were full of the tragedy and the hypnotist was being blamed for the incident, saying the man was still under his influence after leaving the show. They were crucifying him and his bookings were getting cancelled one after another. The club circuit had no wish to allow him to perform under these circumstances. They believed the watch committee of the towns would close them down.

Batley was not to be influenced by the hysterical outcry, but they were in the minority. Martin could not exist with one venue on his side, so he was left with no alternative but to return to his homeland of Australia. The power of the press had drummed one of the biggest talents out of the country. Anyone believing the old adage 'there is no such thing as bad publicity' should study the downfall of this man.

The club was approached by various charities asking for help raising money for many good causes. Always receptive to a worthy cause, every effort was made to help. The artistes loved to get involved. Generally, the maximum an artist worked a night was two hours, so they had time to kill and nothing to do all day. The support acts would do what was called a 'double' with other clubs in the area. If an act was closing the first half of the show at Batley, they would often appear as top of the bill at another club within driving distance, which helped to keep costs down, as both clubs halved the fee. The artistes generally had rather an easy time compared to the average worker. They did their best to oblige with the charity events.

One such occasion was at a mental hospital on the outskirts of Huddersfield. They wrote the most heart-rending letter, asking that a show be put on for the long-term patients who had very little by way of recreation. If a show could be staged during the day it would lighten their lives. I took a trip to the hospital, taking along a technician to establish the feasibility of putting on such a show. The hospital had a remarkable hall and stage area, fully equipped. There were no problems we could foresee so we decided to do the show. The staff at the hospital were delighted by the decision. After taking a couple of weeks to get organised, a date was set.

The hospital staff got beyond themselves and decided to invite the mayor and mayoress of the town to witness this one-off occasion. Together with half of the local council, the press were ready to capture the event. What was not realised was that the hospital was a high-security establishment with doors locked and double locked. The big day arrived and the technical staff got ready for the artistes arrival. However, one of the artistes had a little too much to drink the night before and was late, very late opening the show. The hall was full and the patients, who were normally segregated by sex, were mixed together for this very special event. As the show got more delayed, the patients started fraternising with each other and getting very frisky indeed. It was clear that keeping order was going to be a problem. They were all but bonking each other. It was pure pandemonium.

The dignitaries were all seated, looking very official with their chains of office proudly displayed. I joined them sitting on the front row, waiting for the show to start. Eventually the curtains parted and there stood the singer, opening up the show in an asylum with the song 'Going Out of My Head'. All the dignitaries started shuffling with embarrassment. I was sliding down my chair, disbelieving what I was witnessing. The staff and technicians were in stitches. They could not believe the mayhem. Eventually, all went well after this poor start but it was a show never to be forgotten.

Bobby Caplin, a businessman from Leeds and a tireless fundraiser for the Variety Club of Great Britain, was to meet James to request his help for a very talented doctor who worked for special needs children in Leeds. The doctor had been singled out for recognition as he had diagnosed a child in his care as being deaf. Until his discovery of the true state of affairs, the poor child had been dismissed as being disruptive and educationally sub-normal. A correct diagnosis led to the child being placed in the proper situation, attaining a successful school life. The doctor was recognised as a pioneer in his field and had been invited to attend some important lectures in America. However, although he had permission from his hospital to attend, he did not have the money to go.

He approached Bobby Caplin for help and it was suggested that he ask James as he had heard he had a generous nature. James agreed to do a show and donate the Sunday night to his appeal, thus raising the money to fund the trip. After the meeting, the two men became firm friends, a friendship which was to last a lifetime. Bobby was a constant visitor to the club, he was more like an honorary brother. They were great friends and confidants.

Bobby was the eternal bachelor, having many lady friends but none managing to get the elusive ring on the finger. Bobby had an easy charm and as the friendship grew James placed great trust in him, often confiding his innermost thoughts. There were to be many charity nights at Batley. One such evening was attended by the Duchess of Kent. Jason presented her with a bouquet of flowers. She was so very gracious and Jason was over the moon.

The club worked tirelessly for the Variety Club of Great Britain, whose cause was to help underprivileged children, providing coaches and holidays. Garden fetes, mini-skirt competitions and beauty competitions were all in a day's work for the judges at these events. It was good public relations for all. Generosity overflowed, provided it was a good cause.

Chapter 10
Big Spender

Overleaf: Betty and James.

James and Betty were forever on the road to London: he to see the theatrical agencies entering into contracts for the star billing at the club, she to visit the Chelsea cobbler where her boots were made. Kutchinsky jewellers was another favourite of hers. They were now so famous the doors of London opened to them. They were invited to show business parties, Royal Command Performances and the Water Rats Ball. They were in London so much they decided to buy a mews house where they could stay and entertain their many new friends. Betty would turn the little house into a home to be proud of. Her talent for makeovers was almost as good as her talent for spending money.

They had everything they wanted, but nothing that they needed. What they really needed was peace and harmony. They both had other interests, but this was show business and they put on a good show of being united.

My role at Batley was expanded. James urged me to turn myself into 'Maureen Prest Promotions Agency', leaving me free to set my own agenda, booking artists into different venues but insisting that I be the sole promotions agency to Batley Variety Club. They had first call on my time. I enjoyed the opportunity to broaden my horizons, and was always dreaming up a new story to feed to the press. I put out countless press releases, doing what I could to keep the club in the forefront. It was hard work and time consuming but being part of the 'can do' generation, believing you can do anything if you put your mind to it, I rose to the challenge.

I was not happy with the free ticket situation, at times they were being doled out like confetti. I persuaded James to change to a voucher system. The public could use the voucher to gain entry at a reduced price, turning his half a loaf theory into three-quarters of a loaf. We agreed to trial the idea. It worked and the public used them in much the same numbers as before, but this time we gained extra revenue.

Betty, being the businesswoman she was, wanted to have a meeting with me. Betty knew I was a friend of Pauline but, as the relationship with her husband was now over, I guess she decided my work for the business came before any personal feelings. Her reputation was that of a 'she wolf' so it was with a great deal of trepidation that I met her for lunch. However, we got on well and it was to be the beginning of a friendship. Strangely, James had been the architect of this. I was now part of both camps, with leanings towards James, naturally.

After the meeting I was welcome at the cottage and often discussed club strategy over a cup of tea in the Corrigans' kitchen. Betty encouraged me to take my children Nigel and Chris to meet Jamie and Jason. They all became friends together. Very often my boys would stay over, being taken care of by the babysitters who were always on hand. This arrangement went on for some time until one day I was getting ready to take them to the Corrigans when Chris burst into tears, saying he did not want to stay there ever again. I sat down and talked to him. With tears streaming down his cheeks, his anxiety was very obvious. Between sobs he told me he had heard ghosts and felt them. He was a very sensitive child and was scared of being there. The urgency of his fears had to be taken seriously. After consoling him, I made my own arrangements for the care of my children. They never stayed over again. What Chris was not to know, I too knew there was something strange at the cottage after hearing the many tales Betty had told of the ghostly goings on, tales I had never told my children.

I was celebrating my birthday with James and Betty and a few more guests at the club. The compère that week was an outrageous comedian/singer by the name of John Paul Joans. James and Betty had secretly arranged a presentation for me. After he had performed his act, John called me on stage to receive flowers and a card James and Betty had sent. They enjoyed my deep embarrassment. I was a 'behind the scenes person' and never liked that kind of thing. John sensed my discomfort and, not wishing to prolong my agony, made the presentation with the minimum of fuss.

Later that evening he sought me out and we chatted. He told me that his act had caused problems and wondered if I could help him through my agency as he was unrepresented. He had a fascinating act, the thinking man's comedian, deeply into satire. I decided to take him on. It was to turn into a monumental task. Controversy followed him around like a tame tiger. He was ahead of his time, was a brilliant singer, writer of music and had many strings to his bow. He was a very talented man but wasn't easy to sell, his reputation went before him. An 'alternative' comedian was unheard of in those days. The audiences at Batley loved his humour but alas they were in the minority.

We worked closely together and I eventually became his manager. He recorded a song which he had written called 'The Man From Nazareth'. Mickie Most, who had a record label by the name of Rak Records and was a leading producer at the time, heard the song, liked it and decided to put it on his label. We got a publishing deal and suddenly John's career was taking a different turn.

The record was released around Christmas time. Within a couple of weeks it entered the top thirty of the charts. We went to London, doing radio interviews at the BBC. All went well. John was invited to appear on *Top of the Pops*. It was a huge boost to his career, not to mention mine.

The publishing company wanted a follow up record and paid for a few days stay at the Dorchester Hotel in London; just long enough to get our signatures on a contract. By this time we had become a couple, happy to be in each other's company. We shared my home in Dewsbury. James and Betty were now close personal friends of us both. I continued with my work at the club, also working on John's publicity at the same time. All was going swimmingly. My life had taken a different turn.

Early in 1971, I found I was pregnant. We were over the moon. My eldest son Nigel was now eleven, Chris was eight, we were thrilled at the forthcoming attraction. A baby! Betty was buying little clothes for the event. During the latter stages of my pregnancy, John took a residency at a hotel in Nottingham so he would be near me when the time came. I worked throughout my pregnancy however I had the baby prematurely. It was a boy, weighing in at a little over three pounds. He was very small. We named him Tim, as in Tiny Tim. It had been a very difficult birth. The doctor told me never to have more children, that it would not be a risk worth taking. The new baby was in hospital for many weeks but eventually we brought him home. Nigel and Chris were thrilled to have a baby in the family.

Jackie Trent and Tony Hatch appeared at the club that week and we had a party to celebrate the new baby's homecoming. All friends were invited to our flat in Dewsbury. John had worked many times with Jackie and Tony, on the cabaret circuit. Betty and James turned up, as did Jackie's sister who had a band and worked the clubs. We had a wonderful evening. I could not take my eyes off my new arrival.

Shortly after his homecoming, I had to go back into hospital. John Edwin and his wife offered to take Tim whilst I was away. They loved having him and took great care of him. After returning home, I was soon back at work.

James and Betty were at loggerheads most of the time, James forever walking me around the perimeter of the car park of the club, telling me of his woes. Betty was equally hacked off, but they put on a good show of being together. Betty's bark was worse than her bite, deep down she was a very caring person. She had shown me great kindness around the time of Tim's birth. The trouble was she sent out all the wrong signals, and people misunderstood her.

Their marriage was being undermined by all the back biting. Staff would run to one or the other, telling tales, stirring up trouble between them. If James stepped out of line, Betty would soon know. And vice versa. This couple would stop at nothing to know each other's innermost secrets. They had lost the moral compass years ago. James and Betty were very much alike, they both possessed the driving force of a steam engine. I guess they had to fight their way to the top and had been a good team in the early days, Betty had a good business head and had a sense of mischief about her. She had a deep down sense of fun.

Betty confessed, with a glint in her eye, that when Shirley Bassey was on at the club, she had sneaked into the dressing room during the day, where all the wonderful gowns were hung. She got one of the staff to stand outside making sure she was not caught trying on all Miss Bassey's stage dresses. She was thrilled to bits that they fitted! They were the most wonderful creations, especially designed for Shirley by the famous Doug Darnell.

Fashion was Betty's favourite occupation and she was forever buying the latest designs. Her dress sense became more and more risqué, her evening wear more revealing. Her husband did not approve, making his feelings known. It mattered not, she would be her own person whether he liked it or not. She spent money like it was going out of fashion.

Betty thought it would be a good idea to have an audience sing-song in the interval between the acts, insisting song sheets be printed with all the words for the audience to join in. We all thought she had flipped; it was tantamount to having the song sheet rolled down in a pantomime with the words being pointed out by Simple Simon! She took the idea from the old time music halls, using the same old songs: 'On Mother Kelly's Doorstep', 'Show Me the Way to Go Home' etc.

She insisted on trialling her brainstorm. The staff were underwhelmed as it meant using the old Gestetner printing machine to produce the music sheets. A stencil had to be cut, then loaded onto the machine for printing. Betty was not interested in the complexities, if she wanted a sing-song she would have a sing-song. She had the song sheets placed on all the tables despite objections from James, who hated the idea.

Much to everyone's surprise the first time it was tried the audience loved it. After a few drinks they were more than happy to sing their hearts out, reading the words from the beer-stained song sheets. It meant that the musicians had lost a break, and they had a moan about that, however it made quite a nice addition to the show. Betty was crowing. 'I told you so. The simple things in life are always the best!'

That was rich coming from her. She had everything any woman could want. She was very slim and carried herself well. She was a lady who could turn heads. Her bedroom had a walk-in-wardrobe which groaned with furs too numerous to count. She had outfits for any occasion and the amount of shoes she had almost matched those of Imelda Marcos.

Betty invited me to join her on a shopping trip to London. We travelled in her ice-blue Rolls Royce convertible down the M1. It was a very hot sunny day when we hit the capital, so she put down the hood. We looked a million dollars in the beautiful car. Suddenly, from nowhere, a police car with its blue light flashing pulled us over. We both panicked, wondering what was wrong. The policeman got out of his car, looked around the car we were in, and asked who owned it. Outraged, Betty replied, 'Me!' His eyes lit up. He started chatting her up, asking for a date. We couldn't stop laughing when it became obvious why we had been stopped. She good naturedly bid him 'good day'. Her ego had been inflated. She loved the attention.

Betty talked me into joining her for horse riding lessons. A local stable gave us personal tuition. I had no interest in horses, I simply went along to keep her company. Being Betty, she got the best horse. My horse would follow hers no matter what I wanted it to do. My commands were ignored. Knowing this, Betty kicked her horse into a gallop. I was terrified, clinging on for dear life. This amused my riding friend, the mischievous laugh lighting up her face while mine was a whiter shade of pale. When the horse finally stopped, I could not wait to get off the smelly critter. My feet were made strictly for accelerator, brake and clutch. Trying to make a great big animal respond to the touch of a stirrup was not my idea of fun. Horse riding definitely was not for me. I opted out at the first opportunity.

Betty decided she would build a diner in the car park of the club, something a bit more up-market than the basket meals. She would design and pay for the build, she would be the owner. James was not impressed with the idea but, as always, he conceded to her wishes. His motto had become 'Anything for a quiet life'. She got on with it, designing it along the lines of the American diners she had seen in the States; gingham curtains and tablecloths with a huge griddle where the customers could see their food being cooked. Nothing very pretentious, just honest food and juicy steaks.

It became a popular spot with the artistes who congregated there after the shows. It went down well with the public too as they could rub shoulders with the famous. As for Betty, it gave her another reason not to cook. Not only was it making her money, she could be the best non-paying customer. She very definitely was not a domestic goddess.

If any cooking was done in her kitchen it was the guest artistes doing it, like when Vera Lynn stayed with them. She had been the 'forces sweetheart' during the war and was a household name in Britain. She was a down to earth, homely lady who loved cooking and could not wait to be let loose in the dream kitchen. She made all kinds of lovely chicken dishes for her hosts. James was in his element, not being familiar with the smell of cooking, he really enjoyed the fare. She spoilt him for the whole week of her appearance. He was sorry to see her go.

Eartha Kitt also loved to cook. Unfortunately James was not a fan of the highly-spiced dishes Eartha served up. Politely, he ate up the first time she lovingly placed a dish of something Caribbean before him. After that, he made his excuses, saying he had a meeting or any other excuse he could conjure up to get out of the gastronomic event. His taste in food was very simple, a burnt steak was James's favourite, or, as he put it, when ordering, 'Cremated'. He hated undercooked meat. The diner would be good for him, though he was loathed to admit it.

131

Betty never hired any staff, she simply poached them from the club, with James paying their wages. She was no fool. The diner became James's new office and he spent lots of time there, doing business over a well-cooked lunch.

Chapter 11

Just One Smile

Overleaf: Jamie, James and Rod Price.

In the late sixties, there was a show on television called *The Champions*. It starred Stuart Damon, who played a character called Craig Stirling. He was a very handsome actor, tall and sophisticated. The TV series which had brought him fame had come to an end in America and he was looking for work in England on the cabaret circuit. He was a strong singer and had a good stage presence. The club gave him a week's booking. Whilst he was in town, we took him along with James and Betty to a hospital in Wakefield to open a garden fete.

James drove the Rolls and made a grand entrance into the grounds of the hospital with the celebrity guest on board. We arrived to a great welcome, Wakefield was excited by the prospect of an American star in their midst. The sun was shining, the grounds had been decorated with balloons and bunting. We had a great time helping raise lots of money for the hospital fund. Stuart sat signing autographs, James, Betty and I judged the mini-skirt competition, the skirts getting shorter and shorter. We all enjoyed the day and it made for good public relations.

The Variety Club gave a hand up to anyone with talent. The support acts loved working Batley. They had the comfort of well-fitted dressing rooms and the technical support not available to them in lesser clubs. The circuit of the northern clubs consisted of a chain of venues for the working man. They had concert secretaries who were more interested in playing a game of bingo than the talent they had engaged to entertain their members. Backstage was a cold room often cluttered up with old beer crates and the like. The artistes had to squeeze in a corner to change into their stage outfits. When they did get on stage they were very often interrupted by the secretary calling the audience to order as the pies had arrived, ready for sale.

You may think this is an old joke, alas it was not, it really did happen. All they offered was cold comfort and a damp, beer-stained brown envelope with a hundred pounds for the night. That's if they were lucky. Very often the fee was paid to an agent who booked the concerts. It was never really known how the money was arranged. All in all, the club circuit was a nightmare but it was the training ground for new talent. These poor young entertainers were in the hands of some ignorant concert secretaries who would wrap nothing up. If they did not like the act they would tell them they were rubbish and pay them off. When John was starting out as a comedian, a concert secretary had been so rude about him and his act, he could take his insults no more. John turned to him and said, 'God bless you sir, and may he call for you soon!' The secretary went purple with rage and threw him out by the seat of his pants.

A television producer at Granada by the name of Johnnie Hamp realised the comedy circuit was a shameful situation for the up and coming entertainers. He embarked on a fact-finding mission around the northern clubs. Seeing the wealth of talent and the conditions they had to endure, he decided to make a programme called *The Comedians*. He plucked the unknown comedy workers from the clubs and gave them the opportunity to perform for the mass audience of television. Initially it was a documentary, but it became so popular it took on a life of its own and became a regular series, introducing different comics with each programme.

It has to be said, Johnnie Hamp was the saviour of the comedy heritage which exists in the north. Laughter was always the one abundant commodity. After all, a sense of humour was essential to endure the conditions of the times. Emerging from *The Comedians* came a wealth of talent, catapulted out of obscurity and into the public eye; Charlie Williams, Duggie Brown, Colin Crompton to name but a few.

Charlie Williams was always popular at Batley. Charlie was a one-off, he had been a professional footballer and when that career came to an end he turned to comedy. He was a very funny man and the audiences adored him. On the rare occasions when Batley had been let down by an artiste, Charlie would always step in if he was available. He lived in Barnsley, which was not far away. He could be on stage within an hour. He loved the club and the staff but especially the audience. He loved to make them laugh. So much so, you could almost hear them in the next town.

The Granada television programme had catapulted the funny men onto the best stages in the land. A wealth of talent came shining through, giving them the recognition they deserved. Bernie Clifton was another who stood out from the rest. When James saw him work on the stage at Batley, he took him to one side telling him that his talent was so great he should be managed by the London managements with whom he was now best friends. He took it upon himself to take him to London and introduce him to the top agents who could channel his talents in the best direction. Bernie was forever grateful to the generosity of James Corrigan and the trouble he took, not just with him but with many other artistes James helped along the rocky road of show business.

The London managements had great influence, but they were not always whiter than white. When Frankie Lane appeared at Batley, he and James got on really well. Frankie's claim to fame was a song he recorded in the late fifties called 'Rawhide' which was a big hit in this country, His appearance fee was to be paid direct to the London management. After a good friendship had been struck between the two men it emerged the agency was short changing Frankie. They were returning him much less than had been agreed with Batley. Of course, nothing could be done as other dates had been booked at other venues, but assurances were given that should Frankie appear again James would book him direct and pay him direct.

James was a very generous man. One day, when he learned of the sudden death of a business contact who had fallen on hard times, and knowing he had children and a widow with no means of support, he sent a large cheque to her, saying the money was owed by him to her late husband. It was sent with a message of comfort. James did not owe him any money, it was his way of sparing her feelings and wishing to help at the saddest time in the lives of the family.

James was busy in his office getting through all his many daily messages when a young man requested a meeting. He was a representative for an electrical company. He was shown into his office and James rang down to the kitchen for Edna to send a tray of tea. The young man stopped him in his tracks saying he would like to be shown to the kitchen, for that was the purpose of his visit. He wanted to demonstrate the latest technology in cooking for the catering trade. James went with him to the kitchen. The young man proceeded to set up a high-tech oven, a large catering version of what we know today as the microwave. When he explained to James it worked by radio waves, I think he thought it was something which had come out of the BBC. The young man plugged in the machine and placed a cup of cold water in the oven. Within a minute of switching it on, the cup held boiling water. James and Edna could not believe their eyes. Was this the start of things to come? The age of technology! He could see this would be a great asset for catering in the club so he wanted one there and then. The young man told him he would have to wait for delivery of a new one from the factory. 'No,' said James, 'I want that one.' He could not bear to be parted from it. Naturally, what James wanted he got. The machine was left. It was so funny, James invited everyone who he met to come into the kitchen to see the miracle of the microwave. When demonstrating the machine, he'd put scampi in to heat and usually made it too hot so it burnt his guest's mouth, much to his amusement. He thought it was wonderful that something could be brought to a high temperature without heat! He loved any new inventions, being receptive to the march of progress.

Another time he stepped into demonstration mode was when he had bought a cinema in North Yorkshire. Whilst he was being shown around the premises, he noticed a stack of film tins in the projection room. Soon after he made the decision to buy it, he took a couple of us from the club to see the latest addition to the Corrigan empire. He unlocked the door of the cinema and we stepped into the darkness. James told us to sit down as he went into the projection room to get the projector working, using one of the films which had been left on a pile. He did not know what was in the tins, they had no titles. We laughed and asked what time the ice-cream lady would be around. We settled down to watch the film, which took forever to eventually flicker into life. It was quite a novelty having a cinema all to ourselves. Once the film was running, James came and joined us to watch the most appalling Technicolor film of the battle of Balaclava. At the height of the battle, the wounded soldiers were wheeled into a makeshift operating theatre to be met by doctors who were sawing limbs off the wounded. It was the most blood-thirsty film; we had taken a forty mile journey to see blood and gore. Naturally, James thought it was hilarious that we all felt queasy and refused to watch. He was like a kid in a toy shop, he loved playing with his latest toys, life was fun.

Betty liked playing hostess to the lady artistes visiting the club. Cilla Black amused her with tales of her holiday in Italy. She had bought a beautiful tapestry bag at a fraction of the price one would have paid in London. Cilla told how she carried the bag through customs when returning to Britain. When the customs officer asked her if she had anything to declare, she said 'no' with the most angelic look she could muster. He was about to chalk the new bag clear when she told him to stop, saying it was her new bag and she didn't want chalk on it. She gave herself away. The customs man knew she had bought it in Italy. Poor Cilla, the man took pity and had to smile at her naivety. She got her tapestry bag through customs still in pristine condition without paying the duty.

When Lulu came she brought her mother and younger sister. They looked like peas in a pod and were a most lovely family. Lulu's mum was so youthful and she had clearly passed on her good looks to her famous daughter. Betty was entranced by Lulu, who was fascinated by Buddhism. She kept Betty occupied for hours telling of the magical properties of the fat Buddha she gave her as a gift, a rather garish, ceramic figure. The fat belly and the grin on its face was a token of love and luck. With Betty's disposition to anything mystical, it was given pride of place and the laughing fat man greeted all visitors to Oaks Cottage.

Lulu was fascinated by the well-stocked pantry at the Corrigans, and it must have stuck in her mind. Years later she related her wonder at seeing so much food under one roof when a crew filmed her for a documentary about Batley.

During Lulu's stay, Betty threw a party for her in the club. After the show, a number of actors from *Emmerdale Farm* turned up. The Corrigans knew how to entertain; nothing was spared, it was champagne all the way. The club was turned into the most spectacular party spot when all the patrons had left and the doors had been locked. The musicians were happy to stay behind playing and enjoying the food and drink. The guests went on the oversized stage and partied the rest of the night away, usually leaving as dawn was breaking.

Chapter 12

Y *Viva España*

Overleaf: The logo for 'The Battle of the Knights'.

The Labour government of the day, headed by Harold Wilson, had brought in some pretty tough tax levies for high earners. They introduced a set tax of 98% for every pound earned; six old pence was retained, the government took the rest. Anyone on high earnings was being clobbered by this outrageous state of affairs and it led to the 'brain drain'. A number of artistes left the country, taking up residence in more tax-friendly countries. They were allowed back for ninety days a year and often returned to ply their trade. Other high earners were driven out on a permanent basis. Despite employing the best accountants, the tax bill for the vast Corrigan Ford Enterprise was astronomical and potentially crippling for the business.

The tax situation was also to create other problems for James. The artistes' managements were now asking for the fees to be split: half on contract and the other half in cash. With this obvious tax fiddle, he had to find a pretty shrewd accountant to be able to magic these cash payments away. It was just another headache.

Times had changed, the Labour government saw to that. They had the power of the trade unions behind them and the unions were a force to be reckoned with. They fought for the rights of the working man. The pitiful wages and the harsh conditions of the north had to become a thing of the past; no longer were the workforce to be exploited by the capitalist bosses. The unions were forever in and out of 10 Downing Street, dictating to the powers that be the terms and conditions they had to adhere to if they wanted their support. The Labour government had gained power as a result of the unions dictating to their members how they should vote. 'People power' was taking over from the dark age of exploitation. People were no longer willing to work for a pittance. 'A fair day's pay for a fair day's work' was the motto of the day.

Slowly the pay and conditions improved. People now had more money in their pockets. The face of Batley was changing. The clean air act prevented the polluting smoke being expelled from the many mill chimneys. The air was now clear. Previously, you could see it coming towards you. People's health began to improve. We were walking towards a welfare state, brought about by the Labour government. The man in the street was to be protected.

With the extra money, cars were bought and mortgages were obtained to buy decent housing. The days of the two-up two-down were on the way out. The new housing had bathrooms and kitchens. The tin bath was being despatched to the tip, or the rag and bone man would take it as he made his way up and down the streets. Cooking was no longer done on the cellar head of the terraced back-to-back homes. The people were now so clean they were reluctant to get dirty again, choosing to work in cleaner surroundings than the noisy, greasy mills.

With these improved conditions came a newfound leisure industry. Holidays were no longer spent around the coastal resorts of England. The 'bucket and spade' holiday was no more and travel companies were springing up to offer package holidays for the masses, ready to fly them away to the exotic destinations of Europe. Spain was a favourite.

James and Betty took a family holiday to Majorca. The package holiday business was booming. James was always watching the trends, knowing it was the working class of Britain who spent the most money. He could see what was happening; his relatives on the coast would lose out to the foreign resorts. The money earmarked as pocket money was being spent in foreign lands, which was probably why the government made it hard for money to be taken out of the country by capping the figure at £50 per person. James's cousins who ran amusement arcades in Filey, Bridlington and Scarborough would soon have to settle for the day trippers.

Whilst in Majorca they met a couple who had an interest in a huge piece of land for sale near the coast. The land was situated in the south east of the island and enjoyed long sandy beaches between El Arenal and C'an Pastilla. They took them to see the area. It was flat and close to the beach. It looked a good site. James was mildly interested, knowing the holiday market was on the up. He returned to Batley and over a number of weeks he found himself thinking about the land. He was attracted to the idea of lots of holiday-makers flocking to the certainty of a sunny holiday. This market had to grow. Once there, the holiday-makers would need to be amused. His logic followed that of the coastal resorts around the UK, where the fairground families had now stopped travelling and settled themselves to a more steady way of life in amusing the holiday-makers, for it was they who were the travellers now. His cousin in Scarborough was running a very lucrative bingo and amusement arcade, so lucrative he was now a very rich man. Often he would visit Batley and they would slap each other on the back. They had come a long way from the early days of the travelling showgrounds.

He investigated the tax situation in Spain, it seemed much friendlier to the entrepreneur than England. One paid very little tax in Spain. On the face of it, the idea of developing the land and expanding the business for tax reasons seemed to James the obvious thing to do.

James was toying with the idea of building an enormous amusement park with lots of rides on the Spanish land along the lines of a smaller version of Disneyland. Enclosing the area would be shops which would be sold to merchandisers. The idea of a theme park appealed to James. If he could pull this off, the wheel would turn full circle.

Any profits gained would be virtually tax free. This was the biggest attraction of all as far as he was concerned. He was tired of shouldering the burden of a big business only to hand the lion's share of the profits to the tax man. It soon became clear though that while the taxes in Spain were favourable, very little else was. There were many obstacles to overcome. Should he

145

go ahead with the plan he would have to find a Spanish partner, no foreigner could start a business in Spain without one. Also a Spanish solicitor. The other great concern was the British government limit of £50 per person being allowed out of the country for any foreign visit. This would be a high investment venture and he had to see a way clear of resolving these problems before making up his mind to go ahead.

By coincidence, a gentleman from Morley, an adjoining town to Batley, visited the club and entered into a conversation with James. It turned out he had a business in Majorca. He had bought an old farmhouse with land and turned it into a BBQ night out: spit-roasted chicken, salad and a baked potato, with as much wine as could be drunk. In those days wine cost next to nothing. He was getting coach parties turning up for the all-inclusive meal. It made for a very nice night out. The tour operators took a large piece of the cake but he was still making a good profit. This kind of operation was very smart because in the early seventies, tourists were extremely cautious of being in a foreign country and organised excursions were the only way they would venture out.

The two businessmen were to talk into the wee small hours and James could see how they could be mutually good for each other. After many trips to Majorca, it was decided to go ahead with the plan. A company was set up with the necessary Spanish partner and the land was acquired. Developing it though was easier said than done. Whilst Spain may have been a tax haven, it was a nightmare trying to get planning permission. Permits had to be sought and, in order to get these, a backhander was required. It seemed everything one needed to do was at the expense of yet another permit. You needed a permit to paint a toilet door!

The gentleman with the BBQ business also had a bakery business in Morley. Just as there was a problem getting money out of England, it seemed the same applied to getting it out of Spain. A handy little arrangement had been set up between the BBQ business whereby James would give money to the bakery company in England and collect the same in pesetas on arrival in Majorca. That way, there was a constant flow of funds to keep things ticking over and James avoided being caught with more money than was allowed when travelling out of the country. This arrangement suited both parties; it was the perfect way for both companies to exchange funds. This was good at the outset but when it came to buying the fairground rides, which cost many thousands of pounds, another way had to be found.

The building of the shops was the first undertaking. They were costing much more than had been anticipated because of all the bribes which were involved. Also it was frustrating as the pace of life was so much slower than in England. The heat made the workers slow. One day a workman was painting one of the shops when his paint brush stuck to the surface he was supposed to be painting. James was tearing his hair out at the slow progress. It was costing a fortune to get nowhere.

Once the shops were completed, he sold them off to English concessionaires, thus gaining the money to purchase the dodgem rides, helter-skelter, waltzers and all the other huge pieces of machinery which were manufactured in Italy. Not only did he have the problem of permits with Spain, he had to overcome the same with Italy, again at great expense in bribes. He had taken on a monumental task and it was costing fortunes to make the smallest of progress, but he had started and gone so far down the road there was no turning back. It became a monster, eating more money than could be justified. James was an expert on the battle of Waterloo, but he had well and truly met his with this project in Majorca. It seemed the more money he threw at it, the more he needed.

While James was getting the park up and running, Betty found a penthouse in a quiet little cove, a stone's throw from a beach. They bought it and she furnished it, making them a nice quiet home whenever they were there. She loved the porcelain Lladró figures and collected them, not just for Majorca but for their homes in England. She would buy the exhibition pieces, carrying them back with great care, where they were displayed with pride. They were talking points, so very valuable and very special, adding to the beauty of their homes.

During his trips to Majorca, James would go to a bar in Palma run by an American. The bar was called Jacque El Negro. There he met and became great friends with Freddie Laker of cheap air flight fame. They got on famously, both being pioneers in their own field; Freddie bringing affordable air travel to the masses, James bringing entertainment. The man who ran the bar also published an English newspaper and ran a radio station; he was worth his weight in gold and lost no time in giving them as much publicity as he could. He was to have the favour returned; the park when open would be free advertising for his bar. Also Freddie Laker was happy to tell his passengers a good night could be had at Jacque El Negro's.

There was very little socialising during these times but it made a welcome diversion from the problems. The biggest one of all was how to get the money out of England. James asked a friend to take £35,000 out to the Spanish partner. He was to conceal it in his suitcase and smuggle it in. Things did not go according to plan and the man claimed he was stopped by customs at the airport who apparently found the money and confiscated it. No charges were brought against him for committing what was a serious crime. It was James's belief that he had kept the money for himself. There was nothing James could do but he always believed he had been double crossed. Perhaps he had, but the £35,000 was gone forever.

The park was completed and the 'Carousel de Majorca' was opened to the public. On Sundays the park was heaving with Spanish families bringing in their children to sample the rides. They were spending on candy floss and ice cream. The Spanish are a very family orientated people who lavish everything on their young. That was all well and good on a Sunday, but the next problem to overcome was how to get the people off the beaches for the other six days when the park was almost empty. The tour operators were approached but they were not interested in taking people to a fairground. They felt there had to be more than that for them to sell it as an excursion. There were no chimney pots in Majorca. Had James overlooked the best piece of advice he had ever been given?

James was trying to work out a solution to the problem when he found himself in London at the office of an agent, who was telling him of a new troupe of entertainers. They consisted of well-known film stuntmen who had formed 'The Jousting Society'. They had performed a tournament in the grounds of Windsor Castle and had it filmed in order to get some bookings for an outdoor spectacular. Being stuntmen, they knew how to fall and make the show look authentic. The most wonderful colourful costumes were made together with all that went with a medieval theme: Saracen tents, banners and flags, armour with their own shields. The whole thing looked truly authentic. The stuntmen were so into it they really believed they had been transported back in time and were reliving the battles of old.

It did not take long to get James's attention; he loved all things military, even if this was a bit before his time. He was hooked when he was shown the film. It was action-packed jousting, knights were thrown from their horses and the horses were rolled to the ground. All the weapons were fake but made to look real. They were all actors capable of bringing the past to life, to great effect. This was just what James was looking for.

He got back to Batley and talked it over with me, saying this could be what was needed to bring in the punters in Majorca. It would make a great package to sell as an excursion. The posters could be really colourful and it would be something never seen before in Spain. James was convinced this would bring the crowds who would then visit the fair after the show, spending money on the rides and other attractions.

The job of selling it to the tour companies, promoting and producing it, was given to me. Nothing was beyond the reach of James Corrigan, but no one in his outfit spoke Spanish. 'How can you sell something as big as this when no one speaks the language?' was the first question I asked. 'Oh, don't worry about that, get a translator.' So off I went armed with lots of stills of the intended production.

It took months of foot slogging around the tour operators. Receptions were held in a few hotels where the holiday reps were invited to see the film of 'The Battle of the Knights' as it was now being sold. My task was hard. The culture was so opposite to ours; everything closed at lunchtime and reopened at five in the afternoon when a siesta had been taken and the heat from the sun was once-again bearable. But we had the will to succeed, believing we had something unique to offer. I happily showed the film to anyone who was interested in helping us make a success of the new venture.

On returning to England, we held a reception at the Gore Hotel in London where the press learnt of the latest Corrigan venture. Two of the stuntmen took part in the press reception dressed in medieval costume. The waitresses dressed as serving wenches, enjoying their role of play-acting for the benefit of the press. Some great images had been captured for the following day's newspapers.

I had travelled to London by train, and sat with an agent called Sidney Rose, who was a great friend of the producer of the TV show *This Is Your Life*. James had given me a book by his Uncle Edwin called *Ups and Downs and Roundabouts*, his recollections of the fairground lives of the Corrigans. We got chatting and I told him about the book and how I worked for the great James Corrigan, sowing the seeds of how James would make a wonderful subject for *This Is Your Life*. We arrived in London, me going my way, he going his. I was smiling to myself as I knew he'd make the suggestion to his producer friend. It worked. Within weeks the researchers were on the doorsteps of the club, secretly researching the subject of James Corrigan. I was back in Majorca promoting The Battle of the Knights.

This was to be another of James's ventures which was to cost a small fortune. Anything as big as this coming out of the London agencies came with a hefty price tag. After showing this film around, I pointed out to James that no one had seen these men work. To sign them up without seeing the show live was a giant leap of faith. Also, we all know what happens with filming; there is more film on the cutting room floor than in the can and only the best bits are kept.

As no one had actually booked the show, we had to rely on the film. After this consideration, it was decided to stage the first of the shows in a nearby trotting track rather than go to the expense of building a purpose built arena. If the show was not a success, nothing would be lost. Well, nothing but the cost of the show. It was a huge experiment at this stage.

James, Betty and I were travelling out to Majorca together. I had driven to Oaks Cottage and was to leave my car there and drop my bags off before heading to the bank to get the cash allowance we were permitted to take. We were in the bank for what seemed like ages, the manager insisted we had a cup of tea and biscuits. Well, I suppose with customers this rich, it was a given. Eventually, we all set off and on arrival in Majorca, they dropped me at the hotel on route to their penthouse. I always stayed at the Belvedere Hotel in Palma. They left saying they would return for dinner and a coffee at nine that evening.

When I unpacked the suitcase in my hotel room, I was shocked to see that there were thousands of pounds concealed in every corner. Most embarrassing of all, my underwear had stacks of money hidden in it. I piled it up on the dressing table. I was an innocent carrier of all this currency. Thousands and thousands of pounds.

I was very angry. I guessed the length of time we were in the bank was another of James's well-laid plans. Having someone plant the money and in such carefully hidden items of clothing must have taken an age, for it was not obvious on opening the case that it was stuffed with money. Someone at the club must have taken out all my clothes to do such a good job of concealing the stash. Now a girl has to have some privacy. I dare not ask who had repacked the case, fearing not looking them in the eye ever again. Nothing was out of bounds to James. Had I been caught I would have been chopping salt in Siberia.

When the Corrigan's turned up for their supper, the money was handed over and I vented my anger at them both. James and Betty thought it a huge joke. Betty was in on the plot too, saying that if they had told me I would have looked guilty when coming through customs. You could not stay mad with James for long though, he turned everything into a joke.

That night when the Corrigans had left, I was getting ready for bed, putting on my nightdress, when I was showered with money. Almost a thousand pounds fell out which I had overlooked earlier. I duly returned it the following morning. I had not slept thinking James would think I had kept it back on purpose. When I handed it to him he said, 'Oh, keep it. Buy yourself a dress.' With a thousand pounds! This was not to be the last of the smuggling.

The contracts were about to be signed for the jousting. The jousters' needs came in a list as long as your arm. Twenty horses were to be bought by them, but paid for by James. Then there was the shipping of said horses, together with all the equipment. The jousters were to have a subsistence allowance for the duration of their stay. The leader of the stuntmen was someone well known in the film world, Nosher Powell. He had been in lots of films and was as hard a man as his name suggests. He had a bent nose and looked like a boxer. The cost of the show was £27,000 on top of the many extras, too many to list. It had taken months of travelling backward and forward selling the show; I was sick of hanging around in airport lounges and my children were beginning to wonder who this strange woman was walking in!

On one occasion, I was in the airport in Manchester waiting to fly to Majorca when James got an awful feeling something would happen to the plane. He put out a call on the public address system for me to ring him. Thinking something was wrong, I called the club. He explained his fear, telling me to get in a taxi and come back. I did so because now I was nervous about the flight as well. These Corrigans were a superstitious lot. Nothing happened to the plane. When next I left for the airport I told him that if he any more premonitions, he should ignore them. I could do without all the dramas, life was hectic enough.

Once the show was due to open, someone had to be on site at all times. The day came when the travelling was to end and a permanent home had to be found for me and the children in Majorca. John decided we would do the job together and he came too. When we were preparing to leave, I got a call from James to say he had bought a new pram for Tim. It was obvious he was up to something. I went to the club to see him in his office. I found him on his hands and knees, slitting the plastic material of the pram with a razor blade, taking out the foam padding and replacing it with money. 'No one will ever suspect,' he said.

The pram was packed with notes of the largest denomination he could get. I could not believe the lengths he would go to. He'd probably lain awake at night dreaming up this idea. He worked out that with the child being so small, the pram could go on the plane with me rather than being put in the hold. I could have it with me at all times during the journey. I had to laugh. Needless to say, he was right. No one suspected the toddler was sitting on a fortune. The only trouble was when we arrived in Majorca and the money was removed; the pram was ruined and I was left without a pushchair for my toddler. But who cared, everyone thought it a huge joke. Years later a member of staff from the club told the story to a reporter. They rang me to confirm what they had been told was true. Naturally, I denied it. The story died a death, thankfully.

During the time we were on the island of Majorca, James and Betty came out to spend time in their new apartment. It was a gorgeous penthouse overlooking a quiet bay. They invited John and I out to dinner. We went to a little fish restaurant. The food was unbelievably good. Afterwards, when the bill arrived, we insisted on paying our share. James would not hear of it and said not to worry as it was really inexpensive. How amazing that such a good meal was so cheap. Believing it was affordable, John and I decided to go the following week on our own. When the bill arrived we could not believe how expensive it was. We almost ended up doing the washing up. Another of Mr Corrigan's jokes.

Majorca was not the top of my list of ambitions, being abroad took me away from all I held dear: family, friends and my native north of England. We had taken a newly-built apartment with all mod cons. The trouble was, every time I used anything electrical I got a shock. Having a small child meant lots of washing. If I touched the washer and the sink at the same time, I completed the circuit and the electricity travelled through my body. John loved the cosmopolitan atmosphere. I hated it. Nothing changed, one season ran into another. I remember driving along the Paseo Maritimo, the main road from C'an Pastilla to Palma. It was lined with bushes of rubber plants and poinsettias the size of a house. I remember wishing the leaves would fall as I got so sick of seeing the same vegetation day after day. I longed for the greenery of my native Yorkshire.

My children had been taken out of school on the promise they would be educated in an English school on the island. This undertaking was just another of James's empty promises. His expenditure was so great, any available funds had been swallowed up by the huge undertaking of the park and the show. My children amused themselves by renovating an old pedalo they had found on the beach. Nigel and Chris had the time of their lives playing around all day on the beaches of C'an Pastilla. They never went near a school for months, which did nothing for their education. Eventually I had to arrange their passage back home to be with their father. After many conversations with my ex, it was decided this was in their best interests. They could be back in education, but this was a huge departure from what had been originally agreed. My loyalty to the job was now coming before my family. Once the show was open and taking in money, I could bring them back and pay for the private education we had been promised.

James was sat in the park when he got a message from the club. Thames Television was making a documentary about the early days of the fairgrounds and wanted to know if he was interested in contributing? He was most flattered and agreed. A date was decided upon when he could go to London for the recording. He was to be interviewed in Battersea funfair and asked to talk about the history of the funfairs. They said that as he was an expert on the subject, his contribution to the programme would be invaluable. When he got there, the producer wanted an opening shot of James driving a dodgem car. Being familiar with this fun ride, he lost no time in bumping his fellow riders when, out of nowhere, came a car with Eamonn Andrews in. He stood up with the famous red book and declared, 'James Corrigan, this is you life.' James was whisked to the Thames TV studios where his staff and family were brought on set to tell their anecdotes of the life and times of James Lord Corrigan.

James was totally surprised and hugely flattered by the accolade. They told the story of the opening of the club and his rise to fame. His was a rags to riches story like no other. What James was not to know was that when the programme researchers were gathering information for the show, Betty insisted Con Clusky of The Bachelors should be included as they had performed the opening ceremony of the club. When the researchers mentioned Betty's desire to include the tall Irish man to Allan Clegg, he tactfully explained that if Con Clusky walked on stage to share the moment, James would walk off, television or not. James had long ago realised the importance of Con to his wife. On the 14th February 1973, Gene Pitney, Vince Hill, Frankie Vaughan, Shirley Bassey and Charlie Williams, together with his family and staff, all paid tribute to this remarkable man. Con Clusky was not invited.

The Battle of the Knights was by now almost organised. A venue was found, the extras had been hired as foot soldiers, and musicians were signed up. It was a monumental task bringing everything together. The horses were soon due to arrive and we looked forward to seeing the magnificent creatures.

We waited anxiously in the port ready for the ship to dock.

One of the stuntmen had travelled with the horses, taking care of them on the way across from England. As they came off the ship, we could not believe our eyes. They looked more like donkeys ready for the glue factory. They were nothing like the prancing steeds shown on the film. They looked half dead. Someone had ripped James off, he had paid a fortune for them. Also on the ship was Nosher Powell with his vintage Bentley. He drove around Majorca with a cigar in his mouth like an A-list film star. He was a walking ego. It did not take a genius to work out that we were heading for trouble.

Months of hard work had gone into the presentation of The Battle of the Knights. The show was about to open to a specially invited audience. The Mayor of Majorca was invited along with the head of the army, the police and all the noted dignitaries of the island. There was a priest on hand to bless the show, which was important in a catholic country. I personally thought we needed a miracle not a blessing. I had the unenviable task of coping with all the stuntmen in the run up to the show. I watched them rehearse and thought that unless they could turn things around, it did not look good. There is a saying in show business: a poor rehearsal, a great show. I was relying on this to be true. So much depended on this to turn the fortunes of the Spanish project around.

The most important people on the night were the heads of all the tour operators in Majorca, for it was they who had to be wowed by the show. The whole scheme was built around them. If they liked what they saw, they would be prepared to include the show as part of their summer attractions for 1973, to be sold as an excursion. They knew how important they were. I haggled out a deal with them individually, which took forever. Not speaking their language, I had to work through an interpreter so it was doubly difficult. Also, apart from the language, it was a different mentality. They did not think along the same lines as we. I learned later that Spain, being a catholic country, had large families. When the elders made wills, the farm lands were deemed to be the most valuable and left to their eldest son, who would have been educated. The younger sons were left the coast land. These people didn't have much education and were not the sharpest knives in the box. Suddenly, with the advent of tourism, they were fast becoming millionaires as the coast land was now the most valuable. The big tour companies snapped it up to build the new hotels to cater for the boom in tourism.

It had been a huge task bringing everything together for the opening of the show. The place was packed. James and Betty had brought a party of friends, all excited to see the new outdoor spectacular. I had a little office beside the entrance gate, with shutters to keep out the sun. It was a quaint little building. All the guests enjoyed a drink before the show started, raising a glass to its success. When everyone was seated in the stands that had been decorated in armorial shields, the show opened with all the pomp and circumstance which could be mustered. The knights paraded out looking resplendent in their medieval regalia. The horses' poor condition was covered by colourful tabards.

The show began and from the start it was clear to all that it was an absolute disaster. The knights were falling off their horses before they were pushed. The horses looked too small for the riders. It was the biggest fiasco of all times. I could not bear to watch. I hid in my office by the gate, closed the shutters and sat there wanting to cry. I was absolutely exhausted. The audience were walking out in droves. I could hear the footsteps on the pea gravel as they went. The crunching sound was deafening. What was to be the biggest spectacular turned into something unwatchable. The Battle of The Knights was a huge flop, it was the first and last show. The crushing defeat of failure was a stranger to me. Everything I had worked towards and sacrificed for, the success I so desperately wanted in bringing this show to the holiday-makers of Majorca, was destroyed by these buffoons. Everything was lost.

The actors were paid off and returned to England. This was the last that was heard of The Jousting Society. Everyone was let down by them, not least James. He lost fortunes on the project which was supposed to have been his saviour. It became another nail in his coffin. The money spent on the park and the show could never be recovered, leaving a big hole in the finances of the Corrigan empire.

Feeling so very sorry for him, I told him not to worry about our salaries, just be sure the expense of the flat in Dewsbury was taken care of, which had been arranged before leaving for Majorca. He assured me Stanley Moss the accountant was taking care of the utility bills and everything else.

It took a few weeks folding up the whole unhappy show, after which I was so deflated I left John in Majorca to tie up all the loose ends while I returned home with Tim. I was looking forward to seeing my older children. Thankfully we had got them back in school because, as things turned out, they would not be returning to Majorca.

When I got home there was a warrant for my arrest for non-payment of rates. The electricity had been cut off, as had the gas and the phone. The fridge had defrosted all over the kitchen floor.

After being assured that all was taken care of, obviously someone had been economical with the truth. With very little money, as we had not been paid for weeks, I was in no position to sort out the mess. I got into my car, put Tim in his child seat, and drove to the club. I went round the corner on two wheels I was so angry. I charged into James's office ready for the biggest row, I was furious. Sitting behind his desk was Stanley Moss, the accountant. I asked where James was.

'Waterloo,' he said.

'Waterloo station?'

'No, the battlefield in Belgium.'

Not being able to talk to James, I had it out with Stanley, telling him I had been led to understand he was to sort expenses out but he knew nothing of the arrangement. There was nothing I could do. I managed to telephone John in Majorca and related the sorry tale. John was furious. He got on a plane and came home. He eventually challenged James to sort the mess out. How dare he put his son and me in such an awful position, especially when I had done so much for him. That was the closest I ever came to falling out with James. Eventually he sorted out the mess and all was made good.

I got an irate phone call from Betty. She was ranting on about me having an affair with her husband. What nonsense. I asked her why she thought this. She explained she had just got back from Majorca where in the apartment she had found some eyelash curlers down the side of the settee. I had never been in the apartment, other than when they showed me around. Also, I did not possess a pair of eyelash curlers. For years I had seen Betty bully people but she was not about to turn her venom on me. We had a raging row, cleared the air, and I managed to convince her she was being foolish.

Of course I knew who owned the said curlers. James had met a very beautiful young lady whose family had a holiday home in Majorca. She was Elaine, an ex-model. They fell in love. Once again, she was much younger than James. History was repeating itself. I knew of the relationship but being loyal to James, I was not about to spill the beans. John thought it was hilarious, we had been so busy in Majorca we did not have time for each other, let alone anyone else. As for me being more than a loyal friend and worker to James, that was a huge joke. We had too much respect for each other's heads to be anything other than friends. To be truthful, even that had worn a little thin after the debacle which was Majorca.

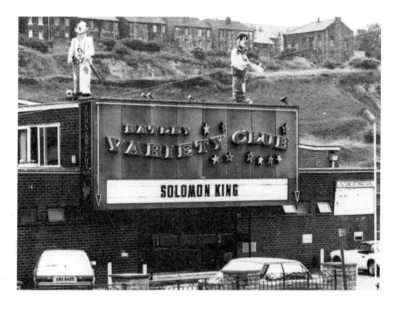

Chapter 13

It's Over

Overleaf: Batley Variety Club at the end of its days.

Betty was holding a party one Christmas Eve and a number of invited guests, together with John and I, had congregated at the house for drinks before going to the club to see the show. It was a very bizarre night. Bobby Caplin was a guest and not Betty's favourite person. Anyone close to her husband was no friend of hers. When the guests arrived in black tie and evening dress, James was sitting in the dining room wearing a sweater. Bobby asked him if he was getting changed. He replied that he was not going to the party as Con Clusky had been invited. When he had been told this earlier in the day, James and Betty had a row. The atmosphere was tense. Betty came down the stairs wearing a long black cloak with a hood over her evening gown, carrying a sword wrapped up as a gift for James and a tray with three black candles. She gave the three black candles to Bobby. James was incensed by this slight against his friend, telling her if he was having three black candles she had better get six for Con Clusky. With that she threw the glass of brandy she was holding at the fireplace, missing Bobby's head by inches. The glass smashed against the wall where he was sitting. That was the end as far as Bobby was concerned, he'd had enough of this woman who was clearly out of control. We all left and the night was spoilt.

The love James and Betty shared had turned to hate. Slowly the dream had turned into a nightmare. They had lost all the respect they had for each other, becoming caught up in an emotional glue pot which neither could extricate themselves from. They had become a couple at war and would stop at nothing to hurt each other. There was the occasional truce, but it was always short lived. James would telephone me at all hours of the day and night, relating the latest row. I could not help other than to lend a sympathetic ear. Equally, Betty did the same. They had created a living hell for each other and it was becoming clear that too much water had flowed under the bridge for forgiveness to take place. They had both been as bad as each other, growing further and further apart. The solution was in their own hands but neither could bring themselves to end the marriage.

Betty would stop at nothing when it came to a fight. She would use anything to score points over her husband. Blackmail was no exception and she never lost an opportunity of letting him know just how tight her stranglehold was. James had always included his wife in all his business dealings, I guess some were of a shady nature, after all you could not go as far as these two without a few skeletons rattling around in the cupboard. They were trapped with each other 'in a well-padded prison' as James put it.

Betty found a sympathetic ear in John. He too was a good listener and tried his best to offer helpful advice. One night John and I had been in bed for a short time in our flat in Dewsbury when the bedside phone rang. It was Betty. She was in a state of agitation, asking me to go round to the house as they were having the most frightful row. I could hear glass breaking in the background. The urgency in her voice told me this was more serious than the usual petty row. I got out of bed looking at the clock. It was two in the morning. John, half asleep, asked me what I was doing. I told him I was going to Oaks Cottage. He was by now getting sick of his and my involvement in the Corrigan rows. He told me to get back into bed and let them get on with it, but something told me I must go so I insisted. 'Well, if you feel like that, I had better come with you,' he said.

When we pulled up to the house we saw the windows in one room were completely smashed. Sally, Betty's mum, was in tears. The house looked like a bomb had dropped on it. Broken glass was everywhere. Beautiful furniture broken. James was sat in his study with his head in his hands. I sat talking to him, trying to establish what had happened. All I could get out of him was how he could take no more. Betty was upstairs. She had locked herself in the bathroom and was drowning herself. Sally was banging on the door, begging her to open it but to no avail. John, realising how dangerous the situation was, went outside and climbed the drainpipe to gain access into the bathroom, which meant smashing more windows. He entered to find Betty in the bath motionless under the water. He dragged her out.

I was downstairs trying to persuade James to go and talk to his wife. All this mayhem was a solution to nothing. I finally got through to him and we started climbing the stairs. As we neared the top, John had opened the door from the bathroom and was walking out with Betty in his arms, stark naked, looking like a drowned rat and pretending to be unconscious. Sally was in a state of collapse at the thought of her daughter drowned. James took one look at the sight of his wife play acting in the nude and in the arms of my partner, turned around and went back to the study.

His rage started all over again. John put Betty into bed. On seeing that her daughter was coming around, Sally calmed down. Eventually all was calm.

The next day an army of people came and cleaned the place up after the devastation of the night before. By lunchtime all the broken windows had been replaced and the smashed furniture removed to be replaced by new.

There was a time when Betty and James had a panic button in the bedroom which connected direct to the police station in Batley. Being so wealthy, the police advised having it fitted for security reasons. They felt they may be targeted by thieves. However, Betty had pressed it so often with the constant domestic disputes the police had got sick of being called out on the many false alarms and disconnected it. I guess John and I had become the panic button.

After the Majorca debacle, I decided to concentrate on John's career. We had a good publishing company and he was doing lots of recordings and was kept busy with cabaret. During this time, the miners were on strike. We both had a social conscience and, feeling sympathy with the miners, we rang Roy Mason, the local MP for Barnsley, offering to help. He was so pleased that we suggested we make a record and donate all the proceeds to the miners' fund. I was still doing bits for Batley, but managed the two projects.

We got really involved with the strike. We went to London and spent lots of time with the leader of the miners' union, Joe Gormley. A local studio offered us some free recording time and John got to work writing 'The Miners' Song'. It was more a monologue with a funky backing. James put some money towards the project and we got the record out in a very short space of time. We had thousands pressed, which we gave to the union in London to sell for their charity. Everyone had given their time and expertise freely. The public were fully behind the strike, we all loved the miners and wanted to help.

Once more, work was taking me away for days at a time from my family. My mother had looked after the children whilst we were away and when we arrived home she told us the phone had never stopped ringing, we were being chased by all the Russian newspapers. It seems the story of the record had gone to the communist country and we had been hailed as heroes for getting behind the workers of Britain.

Ted Heath was now the Conservative prime minister. The miners were winning the strike hands down, the coal stocks which fuelled the power stations were running out. To avoid this, Heath called for power cuts in order to conserve what little stocks they had left. One day I was listening to John's record of 'The Miners' Song' played on Radio 1. The DJ, being a smart Alec, slowed it down towards the end, distorting the voice, saying they had run out of power. I rang the BBC and banned them from playing it, accusing them of distorting an artiste's work, thereby infringing the copyright. Heath had hoped to turn the public against the miners with his power cuts. It did not work. Eventually the miners won a hard-fought battle and brought down the prime minister.

I decided I'd had enough of the show business lifestyle and

wanted a more settled existence for the sake of my children. John sorted himself out with another agent. He still did dates at the club. I scoured around the area, looking for some retail premises where I could open a fashion shop. I found one in Birstall, a satellite of Batley. John and I beavered away, turning an old butcher's shop into what was to become Virgo Fashions, named after my birth sign. We stocked it out. James and Betty came to the opening of my new venture, wishing me luck. It was 1974. The business took off big style. How could it fail? I had the best teacher in the world in James Corrigan.

James and Betty, tired of fighting battles, tried to make a fresh start by buying a yeoman's manor house in nearby Yeadon, Leeds. It was a detached building standing in its own grounds and afforded complete privacy. It was a perfect setting for the armour and battle relics and antiques collected over the years, and far enough away from the club and all the many problems associated with it. Majorca would never attain the financial returns hoped for in the beginning, in fact he would have been better off paying the 19/6 in the pound to the British government than throwing a fortune away on the folly that was Majorca. Hindsight is a wonderful thing.

My new business was doing well and I was about to open another shop. I called in at the club to have a cup of tea with James and to find out what was happening. I walked through the door very smartly turned out. Well, I did have a fashion shop. James remarked that I was looking very affluent. I took the compliment, telling him of my plans for another shop. He looked me squarely in the eye and said, 'Take a bit of advice from me, don't do what I have done. I have created a monster, just do enough to stay comfortable.' The sadness in his eyes told me everything. He was a very unhappy man.

Jamie had met his future wife by now. Oaks Cottage could be their home. Jason was thriving if not gaining height. One night he asked his father why he was so small, James replied a man is not measured from the ground to the top of his head but from his eyebrows to the top of his head, which was a very sweet way of making his youngest son feel good about himself.

Eventually Jamie and his fiancée Janet were married in Hanging Heaton Church, where James and Betty had tied the knot many years before. Their future looked bright. They were a young, good-looking couple with the right values. Having been caught up in the problems of Jamie's parents, they were not about to make the same mistakes as them.

Peace broke out in the new abode in Leeds. The Corrigans were determined to make a fresh start. Deep down they loved each other, even if they did have a funny way of showing it. There was too much at stake for it not to work. They gave it their best shot but, after all, does a leopard change its spots? Betty knew the relationship with Pauline had come to an end long ago. What she did not know was that a new one had started with Elaine.

On the face of it, Corrigan Ford looked to be in a healthy state and Batley was still doing good business, but the artistes were getting greedy. The spiralling costs of the big names were killing the goose which had laid the golden egg. Money was being siphoned off to support the park in Majorca. It was clear something had to give. Then, suddenly, there was no money left. It seemed James had been juggling the finances for many months and it was clear he had sustained major losses, losses which could not be recovered. He was on his way to ruin. The debts were mounting up in Spain and the authorities took a dim view. Unlike the system in England where action had to be taken through the court, there they simply seized any assets against the debts. Betty had secured the penthouse by keeping it in her name, thus saving the property, but everything else was like a house built on sand and suddenly it came tumbling down. Majorca had become James's nemesis. The country was corrupt.

Ultimately, the move to a mansion on the outskirts of Leeds proved to be a step too far. The move brought no more happiness than being together in Oaks Cottage. On top of the debt and the heavy burden of business life, James discovered his wife was now having an affair with his cousin. This was the final straw. He could take no more.

They fought and they rowed, smashing everything in sight. Matters got so bad that Betty called the police and the couple found themselves before the magistrates. Betty brought charges of assault against James, he pleaded guilty to the charges. The court in Otley bound him over to keep the peace. After that, he walked out of the court and out of the club, leaving Betty and Jamie in control. James went straight into the arms of Elaine, who lived in the south of England. Divorce proceedings were instructed and the marriage was all but over except for the formalities. This was 1978, the marriage had lasted almost thirty years. The club had been open eleven years. As far as James was concerned, it had turned into a life of sheer hell.

Betty and Jamie closed the club, then reopened it as a disco renamed 'Crumpets'. This project was to fail after a short time. The world famous Batley Variety Club had closed. The creditors filed for bankruptcy. James was ruined.

Chapter 14

How Deep Is Your Love?

Overleaf: Elaine and James on their wedding day.

For years James had been a tormented soul and now, completely ruined and full of sorrow, he was on the verge of a breakdown. He had given so much to the show business profession and got so little in return. His success had gone global, yet happiness had eluded him. He had provided a venue second to none, the artistes had the benefit of first-class facilities to practice their art, and in return they had sucked the life blood of the club by demanding more and more money, making it impossible to remain viable. James Corrigan had a big heart, gave too much, and when he was in need of help, there was no one there to give it.

James left Yorkshire and moved south to be with Elaine. They were making plans to marry. He loved her very dearly and she was good for him. She was aged 31, he was 53, but it mattered not. They were to be together after all the many trials and tribulations. Their future together looked bright. James was determined to put the past behind him and make a fresh start. He wanted no more publicity and to be allowed to live a private life. He turned his back on Yorkshire, returning only to see his children. He was determined to build a new and happier life, believing he would be back on top within two years.

Elaine and James married in 1979. Bobby Caplin was his best man. By this time the mansion had been sold, together with all the trappings of wealth. The champagne had dried up and they had to start again from rock bottom. James turned his hand to many things but never quite hit on anything that was going to give the couple a good start. His rags to riches story had returned to rags.

James was secure in the happiness that his marriage to Elaine had brought, but the financial insecurity was a challenge. They were to be blessed with four beautiful children; three girls and a boy: Annalisa, Sheralyn, Marilyse and Wesley. They were a normal, happy family, but the finances were woefully inadequate as his children were growing. His ability to return to a meaningful income eluded him. Try as he might, his fortune was not about to return.

It was coming up to Christmas and there was nothing in the bank. They were almost penniless and unable to buy toys for the children. In desperation, James called me, not knowing which way to turn. I suggested we sell his story. We got together and hatched the plan. James made tapes of all the anecdotal stories which he thought would be of interest to readers. I put my promotions hat on and set to work, writing just enough to get some interest going.

Derek Jameson, the then editor of *News of the World*, liked the piece. James and I went to London telling him of the dire situation he was now in. He agreed to buy the story which he would publish in the New Year. We left with a cheque for £800. Knowing he was down on his luck, this was an advance against the story. The balance was to be paid when the story appeared. This was a godsend, as it now provided James with a stress-free time and toys for the children.

We drove back from London absolutely thrilled at the outcome. I then had the task of putting together the full story which we had promised. Unfortunately, Derek Jameson was sacked early in the New Year and the replacement editor was not interested in running the piece. It was panic stations thinking the advance would have to be repaid. The money was already spent. We need not have panicked though; they assured us the advance was to be written off. We heaved a sigh of relief.

Elaine was long-suffering of this awful state of affairs. They moved from one rented house to another, always hoping their fortunes would improve. She was at times exasperated. Her few precious family heirlooms were being sold off to keep them from starving. Try as he may, James could not get back on his feet. He kept in touch with me and I helped him out from time to time. It was unbelievable that someone who had so much could descend to the depths of poverty the way he had. They had no furniture and used garden chairs as a substitute. He was finding it impossible to find his way out of this poverty trap.

He tried so very hard but his business friends had turned their backs on him. He was not afraid of hard work, it was part of his DNA. Whilst living in the south of England he crossed the channel and drove to Germany to buy part-worn tyres and bring them back to the UK to sell for a small profit. After many months of travelling, it covered the expenses and very little else, so he gave up on the venture.

He returned north and leased a road-sweeping wagon, trying his hand at sweeping the streets. Imagine if the press had been aware of this fact, they would have had a field day. They would have revelled in the rags to riches story returning to rags, a great headline for the tabloid press. His Midas touch, which had served him so well in the Variety Club days, had well and truly deserted him.

Twelve years after the close of Batley, James applied to be discharged from bankruptcy and was given a clean sheet to start again. He ventured back into the world of show business and in 1990 acquired a lease on a small club in Wakefield. It only held a few hundred. He called upon his old friends in show business to help him get established again. The club was named Corrigan's but time had run out on the cabaret circuit. It failed in less than three months, returning James back to bankruptcy.

Once more he was in dire straits. As an old friend, he turned to me. We had a mutual friend in Ted Platt. He had been a musician at the club before Freddie Starr whisked him away to be his musical director. I rang Ted, telling him of the hardship James was enduring. I asked if I could see Freddie. Ted said they were due to record a Christmas special for Thames Television in front of a live audience. Ted arranged for James and I to go see the show and he invited us to the aftershow party. I figured that would be my chance to take Freddie aside and tell him just how desperate James's financial situation was.

James and I travelled to London for the show. When we got

there who should be the guest artist but Shirley Bassey. When the show was over, Ted called us backstage and we all went to the bar for the party. Freddie and Shirley were amazed to see James. We all greeted each other with warmth and affection. I had known Freddie long before he was famous; in fact he was one of the support acts who I took to the hospital to entertain the patients on my Wednesday concerts. I knew I could talk to him. At the appropriate moment, and out of earshot, I told him James's true situation. He was shocked to hear how bad things were. I asked him if he would help by doing a benefit concert. Quick as a flash, he agreed. He told me to ask Shirley to do it, I told him not to make her aware, I didn't want to put James through the embarrassment of her knowing the truth. Shirley was so pleased to see her old friend. They enjoyed chatting together and she invited James to her hotel for lunch the following day.

Freddie could not believe James was so broke. He had given so many people a hand up in show business, including himself. When Freddie first appeared at Batley, he was unknown. He thought it was the least he could do to help out now.

The benefit concert took place at Roof Top Gardens in Wakefield. James and Elaine turned up for the show. Tickets were sold out and we made lots of money. To his credit, Freddie paid all the artistes and musicians who took part in the show out of his own pocket. Whatever James did with the money was to no avail, weeks later he was broke again.

Chapter 15

Pennies From Heaven

Overleaf: James at his coin stall in York.

The two years James had predicted it would take to return to good fortune was turning into many years. During this time his family was growing up and the poverty they endured was taking its toll on his marriage. Sadly, in 1992 James and Elaine were to separate and would later divorce. They had suffered thirteen long years of sheer hardship. James never stopped loving Elaine and, despite their separation, they always remained friends. The children of the marriage, three daughters and a son, were a great credit to them. They had been brought up with impeccable manners and spoke beautifully. They were all of school age and doing well.

James was thankful for the years spent with Elaine, though deep down he always knew the age gap was too great and this became more apparent as time went by. What was of no consequence when they married had become important. He had now reached 67 years of age but Elaine was still young and beautiful. He was happy to make way for her to find happiness with someone new.

James went to live in York. He made a living selling old coins on a stall in York market. He was not far away from his family who were based on the east coast. They could catch a bus to stay with their father, and often did. The children loved staying with him and exploring the lovely city of York. James would also visit them as often as possible. With their new arrangements, James and Elaine shared the parenting.

Jason, James's second son with Betty, was now a young man. He was a troubled soul, the victim of the break up of his parents, but he tried to live a happy life. However he had more to cope with than the wreckage of his parents' divorce; being of impaired height he always felt at a disadvantage. Eventually he was to spread his wings, living an independent life in his own flat near to his mother. He was managing very well. He took up a college course and he studied hard but tragically, in 1997, Jason was found dead. He had died suddenly. A post-mortem revealed he had died of natural causes. Jason was a young man, a whole life before him. The family were devastated by the loss of a much loved son and brother. The Corrigan family gathered for the funeral. The loss was too great for Betty and she became a recluse, finding no peace from the pain of the loss.

When the press discovered James was living in York, they tracked him down and made contact with him. He arranged to meet them in a pub for a chat. A reporter and photographer turned up to get a story but as they stood in the bar chatting away about old times, James got the distinct feeling he was falling into a trap. The press, judging by the questions they asked, had obviously been waiting for the downfall of James Corrigan. It was clear they had this as their agenda. As they left the pub, the photographer asked James to sit on the pavement while he took a picture of him. His intuition had been right. James told him to piss off, knowing the caption for the picture would read 'James Corrigan in the Gutter'. The photographer left without his picture.

James lived in the pokiest little flat called Halfpenny House. Its name reflected the austerity of the place. It consisted of one room with a tiny kitchen and bathroom. It was a most depressing place in the shadows of York Minster. He had a door that opened on to a tiny garden. He loved feeding the squirrels who came to see him every day and he shared what little he had with his wild friends. He loved watching their antics. With lots of friends around the town, he was happy enough.

The American visitors to the ancient city of York lined up to buy the coins. Once again he had found a niche market and no doubt gave out all the information of the life and times of whatever century the coins had been minted. Although he never made a fortune selling his coins, he enjoyed anything historical, and what money he made went to his family.

At the age of 72, James was having trouble swallowing. He was diagnosed with throat cancer. The prognosis was not good. He was devastated for he had not given up hope of making enough money to see the children and Elaine comfortable. He felt guilty that she had given up so much for him and he had not provided her with the creature comforts she so richly deserved.

When it was learned James Corrigan was terminally ill, the people of Batley wanted to help. Knowing he had a wish to take his children on the holiday of a lifetime, they sprung into action and arranged a benefit concert. The local paper, which had been so reluctant to offer any coverage when the club was at the height of its fame, could not do enough. They approached me to put the show together. Again I put on the hat of a promotions manager, contacting as many artistes as possible, requesting they send messages of goodwill. The jungle drums were sounding. I rang artistes of the past to come together to take part in a show in Batley Town Hall. We would have held it in the Batley Variety Club, which by now was called The Frontier and was run by Derek Smith, an ex-employee of James who had worked at the club in its hey day. I approached him to use The Frontier to host the benefit concert and his response was hostile to say the least. I wanted the floor to open up and swallow me whole. Despite Derek's big claims to his contribution to the club at its height, he wasn't prepared to return the favour James had given him. Still it was his loss, as the show was being televised. He was to lose out on a great deal of publicity.

Betty was invited, James and Elaine being guests of honour. His children took their seats beside their parents. The place was packed to capacity. All the proceeds went to James. Roger Keech, a director for the BBC, covered the night, making a documentary of the occasion. It was a night to remember, tributes came flooding in: Shirley Bassey, Cliff Richard, Frankie Vaughan.

The Water Rats charitable organisation very kindly sent a nice cheque. James had given them a great deal of money in his time and they were returning the kindness. Bobby Caplin, his dear friend, was there to raise as much as could be mustered. The New Bachelors topped the bill. Con Clusky and his brother Declan had by now split from John Stokes, the third member of The Bachelors, and it was John who brought his new act to perform for James. Also Bernie Clifton, The Grumbleweeds and many more, all joined by the original musicians from the days of the Batley Variety Club.

And so it went on, all paying tribute to a great man. At the end of the performance, James and Betty were invited onstage to receive an award. The mayor of Kirklees presented him with a plaque. His award read, 'To James L Corrigan on behalf of the people of Batley, in appreciation of his outstanding contribution to the field of entertainment in creating the world famous Batley Variety Club.'

Not wanting to leave Betty out, a local gift shop had donated a limited edition dish, which the mayor also presented. On receiving this, James gave a speech with Betty at his side, giving her credit for all she had done for the club. At last they stood side-by-side, each acknowledging the great parts they both played in the birth of the most famous club in the north of England. At last they were burying the hatchet. It was a very moving occasion.

Betty was delighted to meet James's children. She sat chatting to them. The audience had been overjoyed knowing they had helped a man who had done so much for the area. After the show, James turned to thank me, telling me I should be very proud of myself for pulling it all together. 'Didn't you teach me all I know?' was my reply. This show took place in December 1998, the BBC named the film *Batley, King of Clubs* as a tribute to a special man who had done so much for the area. With vision and flair, he had catapulted Batley onto the world's stage.

Strangely, neither the town council nor the local press ever acknowledged the great service he had done for the area and the local businesses, for all they had gained from his vision and foresight. Whilst it is true he could never have a blue plaque honouring his birth place, being of a travelling family, the council should have made some civic gesture to honour the great service he bestowed on the little town of Batley.

James and I had always been friends. For years he rang me every morning at 8.30 without fail, just to have a chat. Always cheerful, his good humour never deserted him. He would start the conversation by saying, 'Now then chicken, how are you?' Over the years I knew what was happening in his life and he knew what was happening in mine. After the split with Elaine he often came to my home and occasionally stayed over.

On one occasion we went to see Pauline, his old flame, who was now enjoying a long and happy marriage with John, an ex-police inspector. They made him very welcome in their beautiful home, furnished throughout with cream carpets. When we left James said to me, 'I think she should have silk ropes around that place.' He was scared of spilling his drink on the carpet. Just for old times' sake I took him to see Pauline's mum. Everyone made him welcome.

James Corrigan's story never lost its lustre. We were invited to take part in a show for Yorkshire television called *Magic Moments*. We were asked to relate our times during the heyday of the club. When the presenter, Christine Talbot, asked James who he had paid the most money to, he replied, 'My ex-wife!'

Taking part in the same show was Brotherhood of Man, a group who won the Eurovision song contest back in the day. James had booked the group long in advance of their win, but their appearance at Batley followed the contest. The lead singer in the group approached James to ask for more money than had been contractually agreed. It was pointed out that had they lost they would have been paid the agreed fee. 'But we won,' said the singer. James told them that was his good luck and not theirs. As we all sat in the green room of Yorkshire Television, we were all polite enough not to mention the incident and got on with relating our different stories in front of the cameras.

James took part in many interviews revisiting his great achievements. One such reporter was Ian Clayton, well known for his down to earth, homespun style of reporting. A magical interview took place in front of the fireside in my home in Yorkshire. Before the crew turned up, James had asked me to make them sandwiches and cakes, for this was his way. He had been brought up with good manners and a strong belief that a Yorkshire welcome came with a good strong cup of tea served in a cup and saucer, preferably china. And a biscuit.

The crew arrived and Ian settled down to interview James, who was relaxed. He wore the weary lines of a face knowing more than most. Strangely, James did something he'd never done before; he went back to his beginnings. He had spent a lifetime putting his past behind him, bettering himself every step of the way. Was it Ian's respectful, easy charm which took him back to the place where his life began at his grandad's knee, telling him of the advice given many years before? 'Go where the chimney pots are!' Ian's eyes widened. He was mesmerised by the man he had before him. James knew he was not long for this life and perhaps knowing this, Ian was to see the real James Corrigan. It was the best interview he ever gave and it was to be his last.

Despite the hardships of the years following the closure of his many businesses, James never lost his sense of humour, always having a laugh and a joke, his spirits stayed high. He was ever the showman, still dreaming up new ideas. He was a self-confessed ideas man with the courage of his convictions. A rare breed.

In May 1999, I was trying to get James into some decent housing and away from Halfpenny House. York social services were sympathetic towards his cause and agreed he needed help. I arranged to meet him in the famous Betty's Tea Rooms in York and then to go with him to social services to discuss his relocation. Before we met, I saw in a newspaper that James's ex-wife Elaine had won £2.2 million on the National Lottery. When we met up in the tea rooms he was thrilled, happier than I had seen him in months. I asked him what Elaine had done with ticket from the Saturday night to claiming the prize on the following Monday? I had always wondered how much importance a scrap of paper would assume and what you would do with it for what would seem like an eternity before you could claim the prize two days later. 'It was in my wallet,' he said.

I looked at him. 'Hang on,' I said, 'If I am divorced from you and have just won 2.2 million pounds, my ticket would not be in your wallet!' He threw his head back and started laughing. 'I knew I couldn't fool you,' he said and then told me what had happened.

James had been staying with Elaine for a few days. Before leaving and returning to York, he asked his eldest daughter Annalisa to go to the shop to buy three lucky dips for the weekend's lottery draw. She obliged and James put the tickets into his wallet, kissed everyone goodbye, and returned to his home in York with his youngest daughter, Marilyse, who was a bit of a daddy's girl and loved spending time with her father. It was a spring bank holiday weekend. James was checking his ticket as the numbers were being drawn on the Saturday night. He had all six numbers. He'd won the jackpot. He sat looking at the ticket, thinking what to do. James Corrigan was working out how to deal with the win.

He rang Elaine and told her to come to York, explaining how the last hour was about to change their lives. He had a cunning plan. She drove to James and they decided she should claim the money. He was terminally ill and was afraid that most of the proceeds would go to the tax man if he claimed it. He had no intention of letting them take another fortune from him.

Just as he had made the first fortune from bingo, he was to get a second as a beneficiary of the game. Dame fortune had most certainly been a friend to James. His wish to make sure Annalisa, Sheralyn, Marilyse and Wesley were well taken care of before he left this earth had been granted.

James gave one million pounds to his eldest daughter who had bought the ticket. The rest was shared, buying Elaine a luxury house. He asked me to return the money which the Water Rats had sent on the night of his benefit concert. I did so, saying his fortunes had changed, he was happy to return the money in the hope it would help someone else who had fallen on hard times.

Elaine and the children were now in a position to get what she had always wanted for them; a place of their own. The house they settled for was in a little village on the outskirts of Beverley, a very pretty part of North Yorkshire. It was an imposing property with its own lake, a wood, and lots of outbuildings to keep horses.

James bought himself a house down the road from Elaine's luxury home, saying goodbye forever to Halfpenny House. They were all very comfortable and, most importantly for James, close together. His children now had the little luxuries in life that they had thus far been denied. This made their father a very happy man.

I joined him most weekends, helping him make a home for his visiting daughters and Wesley, his young son. Two of the bedrooms were chosen by Marilyse and Sheralyn.

We set about getting furniture and soft furnishings, turning them into the most wonderful bedrooms a girl could wish for. We both enjoyed scouring the shops to get the little soft touches to finish off the now perfect rooms. The girl's beds had been draped in the fabric of the curtains which I had sewed for them. Whilst out shopping one day, we came across a beautiful china musical carousel, it was exquisite, James had to buy it. He placed it lovingly in the bedroom Marilyse had chosen. It held more significance to him than could be told. Mementoes of the fairground were never far away from James.

In his regular 8:30am phone calls he usually had a list of things he had thought of to add to his new home. I would buy them and take them on my next visit. One morning he asked me to get a computer for Wesley, saying he would pay me the money when I delivered up the treasure for his son. He loved making the children happy.

The new domestic arrangements worked well; Elaine called everyday to see him, with the children forever in and out. My weekends were taken up with visiting James. I would take him to the car boot sales. He loved rooting about in them, trying to find some treasure. I made him meals which he could tolerate. It was getting harder for him to swallow; the cancer was beginning to overwhelm him.

His eldest daughter Annalisa was preparing to marry in the south of England. James was looking forward to being the father of the bride, proudly giving her away and playing his part in the ceremony. As the date drew nearer, it was clear James was not strong enough to attend. He called on best pal Bobby Caplin to represent him on this special day in his daughter's life. Bobby was the perfect stand in, performing his role on behalf of James. He made a wonderful speech. The day was a sunny and very happy occasion, marred only by the absence of the bride's father. When the video of the ceremony was shown, the soundtrack was from none other than Louis Armstrong singing 'We Have All the Time in the World'. The happy couple may have had all the time in the world to look forward to, alas James's time was running out.

James and I would sit and talk of old times. He turned to me one day and said, 'Didn't we have fun!' His life had been remarkable, mine had not been without its moments. We had stayed friends throughout the ups and downs. I remember saying to him, 'One day you will be a legend in your own lunchtime. You should write a book.'

'Why don't we?' he said. The royal 'we' again, meaning me!

'Let's start at the beginning,' I said, 'what was your father's name?'

'Joseph,' he replied

'And your mother's name?'

'Mary!'

'Calling you Lord!' I exclaimed. 'Well James. I think it has been done. Not only that, it was a bestseller!'

We laughed and got no further with the story.

In the summer of 2000, Danny La Rue was doing a season in a theatre in Bridlington, which was not far from James's new home. James made contact with him to renew the friendship they had shared many years before when Danny was his guest at Oaks Cottage in Batley.

Danny insisted that James bring his family. Pauline, John and I all went along too. Danny was thrilled to see us. During the show, Danny announced to his audience that the famous James Corrigan was in the house. The audience stood and applauded. Danny was moved to tears; he was still wearing the beautiful watch James had bought him all those years ago after his run at Batley.

The two men spent time together after the show catching up. No one would have known the hardship James had endured in the years between. He was a proud man, with dignity. Despite being seriously ill, his happiness was clear to see, being with an old friend, sharing old times. His children from his marriage to Elaine were not to know the dizzy heights he had reached. He was just their father. They loved him dearly, never knowing the fame and riches he enjoyed before they were born. Their riches were the closeness of their father, the part he played in their formative years which was denied to his first family.

James was seeing his eldest son Jamie on a regular basis. Jamie carried the scars of neglect and the unhappiness from his early years but all that was behind them now. They spent many happy hours together reminiscing about old times. James asked Jamie to promise that when his time came, to take his ashes to the special place on Hull fairground that every year was the spot at the end of the rainbow for the Corrigan family. It marked the beginning of a rest at season's end, away from the hard work of the fair, if only for a few short weeks.

James died in the arms of his family in December 2000. His life had gone from rags to riches to rags and back to riches again. He died as he had lived, a millionaire. Almost two years after his win, Jamie carried out his father's last wishes, burying his ashes for eternal rest in his own little spot, his rainbow's end in Hull fairground. His work was done.

A traveller who had travelled somewhere over the rainbow, the world will never see the likes of him again; a man who had the heart of a lion and the charisma to eclipse the sun. During his time on earth, he brought happiness and entertainment to so many, gave respectability to a grimy little mill town and placed it firmly on the map through the medium of show business. Batley Variety Club was indeed world famous!

Maureen Prest was the promotions and public relations manager for Batley Variety Club 1967-1974. She was a close friend and confidant of James Corrigan, the founder of the club.

Maureen has worked as a theatrical agent, artist promoter and record producer. After leaving show business in 1974, she launched a successful fashion business with multiple outlets.

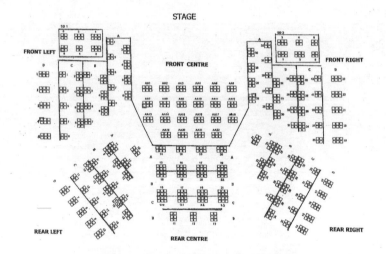

For more on this book visit:
www.kingofclubsbook.wordpress.com
www.route-online.com